"Kudos to Carrie Fox for includir
foundational principle to powe
She advises the reader to be a "radical listener" to go
beyond surface elements into much deeper discovery to
build a trusted relationship with stakeholders for effective
engagement and impactful action. *More Than Words* is
overflowing with insights and guides the reader to embrace
principles to activate profound change."

—**Carol Cone**, *CEO, Carol Cone ON PURPOSE and
author of* Breakthrough Nonprofit Branding

"*More than Words* is a deeply thoughtful book, full of practical
wisdom, for anyone who seeks to communicate effectively to
share ideas, build trust and create a better world."

—**David Bornstein**, *Author of* How to Change the World,
*award-winning journalist and
Co-founder, Solutions Journalism Network*

"Carrie Fox says it best: communications can be one of the
greatest levers for change. Yet, she also reminds us that the
people behind the words, as well as those impacted by them,
must also be considered in order to create ethical social impact
rooted in solidarity. *More Than Words: Communications
Practices of Courageous Leaders* is filled with stories,
actionable strategies, and wisdom to do just that."

—**Professor John Trybus, Ph.D.**, *Executive Director,
Georgetown University's Center for Social Impact Communication*

"Carrie Fox marries profound boldness with deep inclusion in
all of the work she does. She is unmatched in her ability to
help those on the frontlines of social change lead with stories
and vision that can move the world towards a more just and
flourishing future."

—**Josh Stearns**, *Senior Director, Democracy Fund*

"Carrie Fox delivers just the right mix of practical guidance and big-picture wisdom. *More Than Words* is a must-read for anyone who wants to make more of their role as a communicator for change."

—**Mark Van Ness**, *Founder, Real Leaders*

"I've experienced Carrie's brightness and heart work as a client. She delivers impactful strategic communications as a consultant. With this, *More Than Words: Communications Practices of Courageous Leaders*, Carrie has scaled her brilliance via a keepsake filled with wonderful wisdom nuggets. What a remarkable debut for an extraordinary, badass woman leader."

—**Ken Walker**, *Executive Vice President, Diversity, Equity, Inclusion & Culture, Per Scholas*

"Carrie Fox walks us through her own growth journey, making the challenges and the a-ha moments relatable. The questions and exercises she suggests in the book are designed to push readers along their own growth journey of understanding and ability to implement change. Carrie's book is very useful for anyone open to change but unsure how to start or anyone already on the path wanting to push themselves further."

—**Stephanie Ettinger de Cuba, PhD, MPH**, *Executive Director, Children's HealthWatch*

"*More Than Words: Communications Practices of Courageous Leaders* is a must-read for anyone looking to unlock their potential as a communicator for change. Carrie leads us on a journey through her own experiences to help us tap into the power of communication and drive positive change in our personal and professional lives. This book is a comprehensive guide to effective communication that is both inspiring and empowering."

—**Fern Fernandez**, *CMO to top global brands*

"*More Than Words* guides communicators to create a more inclusive and accurate representation of the world. Fox's positive message centers around acknowledging privilege, breaking implicit biases in storytelling, and using communication to disrupt cultural norms. She emphasizes the importance of asking thoughtful questions and gives us hope that all of us can become more effective communicators. Fox highlights the importance of understanding one's communication style, being authentic and specific in storytelling, and actively seeking out diverse perspectives. By practicing effective communication and reflection, positive change can be achieved."

—**H. Art Taylor**, *President and Chief Executive Officer, Better Business Bureau's Wise Giving Alliance*

"Carrie Fox has a way with words, and a way with people, and a way with purpose. As you can see from the wisdom in these pages, she uses these considerable talents and applies thoughtful and meticulous care in supporting mission-driven leaders and organizations in saying what we mean and meaning what we say. Carrie's insights are both a flashlight and a spotlight—helping us to light the path ahead and also to give center stage to our vision."

—**Schroeder Stribling**, *President and CEO, Mental Health America*

"I'm a firm believer that powerful communication starts with deep listening — not just to words and ideas, but also to emotion, energy and body language. Carrie is the exemplar of a great listener. She has the ability to track multiple signals, translating them to incisive questions that help people feel truly seen."

—**Jennifer Brandel**, *Co-founder and CEO, Hearken*

"Carrie Fox's *More Than Words* reminds us all that what and how you communicate makes a difference. Her encouragement to *be the leader we need* resonates with a sense of urgency these extremely polarizing times. This book along with Carrie's encouragement to be bold and aspirational with your team and stakeholders has never been more important. Carrie provides strong leadership and has shared not only the spotlight but also ownership with her team. She has set a powerful example for those who are committed to equity and inclusion and provided a set of tools in this book that will assist all who are on this same journey."

—**Lori Little**, *President and CEO,
National Affordable Housing Trust*

"Carrie is my go-to source for trusted counsel because she listens intently to understand and values the responsibility we carry as communicators to produce strategic messaging that inspires action for good. Now readers everywhere can learn from her collection of lessons to gain courage as leaders and experience the joy of crushing any communications challenge with purpose, kindness, and grace."

–**Nancy Newton**, *Vice President of Public Relations*

"Carrie leads with grace, compassion, and courage in everything she does—and this book is no different. For 20 years, she's brought a servant leadership mindset to her work that has helped to cultivate rich conversations, meaningful relationships, and lasting social impact. Regardless of where you are in your growth journey as a communicator, this book will push you further."

—**Bill Milliken**, *Founder and Vice Chairman,
Communities In Schools, Inc.*

"Carrie Fox understands the infinite potential of story. Many good communication consultants can help you shape your story, but Carrie actually helps you find your story--the truly authentic one that connects your work to its larger purpose; one that you might not even realize exists. She asks the hard questions that challenge you to articulate where your heart and values live within the organizational structures you have created. When we first engaged Carrie over a decade ago, we thought it was to help us become better communicators, which she did. More importantly, she helped us become better leaders and, because of that, better people. Carrie is a visionary in the field of mission-driven communication, and we are so lucky that she is part of our story."

—**Deb Gottesman**, *Founder and Co-Executive Director,*
The Theatre Lab School of the Dramatic Arts

"Carrie Fox is a changemaker. Throughout her career and life, she has refined her unique ability to advance social change through communications and storytelling. Her natural curiosity and a palpable passion for social justice authentically fuel her communications and strategy. Carrie uniquely blends the art of coaching and inspiring in all her interactions, with clients, teammates, and now, readers. Those of us on the receiving end of her efforts are far better for it.

—**Carolyn Berkowitz**, *President and CEO,*
Association of Corporate Citizenship Professionals

MORE THAN WORDS

COMMUNICATIONS PRACTICES OF COURAGEOUS LEADERS

CARRIE FOX

"Overflowing with insights,
More Than Words will guide you to embrace
principles that can activate profound change."

CAROL CONE, CEO, CAROL CONE ON PURPOSE

Cover and interior design: Anne C. Kerns
Author photo: Damith de Silva

ISBN: 978-1-7346186-2-4

Dedication

To the curious and the courageous.

Contents

"Do the best you can until you know better. Then, when you know better, do better."

DR. MAYA ANGELOU

Introduction

Grounding

The year was 2010. The United States was coming off what had been coined the Great Recession[1] as President Barack Obama was entering his second year in office. The U.S. economy struggled to return to early 2000s economic numbers, as homelessness remained an ongoing concern in major cities. Healthcare costs were rising, and food insecurity rates remained the highest on record[2].

Meanwhile, in Washington, DC, hundreds of volunteers gathered for a national service event. Their mission was to fill thousands of care kits for people experiencing homelessness and food insecurity. Any participant scanning the crowd could see that the volunteers were engaged. News coverage was plentiful. The beneficiaries of the day's packages would soon receive a nice meal with a handwritten letter enclosed. By all accounts, the event was a success.

When the leader of the day took to the stage, he shared his gratitude for the group and his enthusiasm for the energy he felt in the crowd. He celebrated the participants for hitting the day's goal. Then, he invited everyone to return in a year's time to double the number of care kits they'd just filled. Soon enough, the production lines would begin again.

The crowd cheered. And that is where this story begins.

For so long, organizations have unwittingly connected their purpose to production. A lofty, ambitious goal is set, and everyone involved begins their work toward that goal, often without acknowledging what is happening on the broader stage of society. Words set the tone, and actions follow.

In this common scenario, it becomes unclear if an organization is working to alleviate social issues or perpetuate them. **Is our aim to increase the care kits or reduce food insecurity? Do we want to challenge and disrupt inequities or co-exist with them?**

It comes down to how we communicate.

Whether you're trying to drive an organization to more equitable outcomes or are thinking about the role you individually play on a team, your good thoughts and well-intended actions may lead to unintended consequences. This book will help you realize your power as a communicator and show how directly *you* can impact an outcome.

How do I know? Because I've lived this work for the past twenty years, supporting hundreds of organizations as a social impact communications consultant.

In 2004, I launched a communications firm called C.Fox Communications. Our goal was to work with organizations desiring to tell important stories but with limited resources to tell them. We brought our best-in-class PR, marketing, and messaging skills, honed from years of working in public affairs, on Capitol Hill, and on national and global purpose-driven brands, to support hundreds of organizations advancing their missions effectively. Often, our work intersected directly with an organization's fundraising and development function, and the words we'd craft would turn into an organization's annual appeals and calls for donations.

We did this work well. And we did it for many years—until I couldn't do it anymore.

One day in 2016, at the height of Presidential debates between Donald Trump and Hillary Clinton, it became all too clear that the stories American society had been telling for decades—stories and narratives reinforced by those in the greatest positions of power—were also reinforcing and perpetuating harmful narratives about race and class. Portrayals about the systems and norms that I had taken for granted were further driving divides between how we understand and connect with one another.

It was then that I started to connect the dots back to my own work—the words I had used to support nonprofits in their mission-moving efforts and the organizational decisions that those words had influenced. I had seen the unintended impact of my work, and there would be no unseeing it.

So, I decided to make a change—and a significant one at that.

Shortly after watching those U.S. Presidential debates, I felt a calling to close my company. I had lost my inspiration and found myself on autopilot. I realized I had become part of the problem.

So, I dared to ask, *what if* I started all over again, from a place of truth:

- *What if* we leaned on the hard skills of communications to shift harmful narratives?

- *What if* we could meaningfully disrupt inequities in organizations—including our own—rather than continue to co-exist with those inequities?

- *What if* we could improve broken or failing systems by tapping into courageous communication as a change management tool?

The call was strong, and the timing was right. I had been watching organizations struggle with how to communicate and follow through on their commitments toward social justice. The problem, I found, wasn't the lack of communications resources. Rather, it was uncertainty about how to communicate with care, courage, and clarity during challenging times.

A willing partner in the journey—one able to speak truth to power with love—might just help.

In January 2017, I opened the doors to Mission Partners with a clear commitment to using communication as a powerful force for good. Just one year later, we became a Certified B Corporation™.

WHAT IS A B CORPORATION?

Certified B Corporations, also known as B Corps,
are committed to using business as a force for
good. They are willing to have their practices
independently vetted by a third party and to
make their results transparent. B Corps undergo
a rigorous certification process to improve their
social and environmental performance. They
don't just say they're good businesses or socially
responsible businesses; they're legally held to
higher social and environmental performance
standards.

You can see the score of any B Corp, including
Mission Partners, on the B Corp directory site
www.bcorporation.net/en-us/find-a-b-corp.

With eyes wide open, hearts on our sleeves, and minds at
the ready, we grounded ourselves as true mission partners:
guiding organizations and their leaders while helping them
fill knowledge gaps and community divides.

Each day, we think carefully and intentionally about
the guidance we deliver to our clients and the power of our
words in informing actions, beliefs, and understanding of
issues—from the role of vaccines on public health to the role
of technology and social media platforms on democracy.

We help organizations understand and articulate their
commitments as a way to drive real and positive impact in
their respective communities. And we apply the same rigor
to our own organization.

Mission Partners is a women-owned and women-led community of thoughtful and passionate communicators guided by the following values:

- **We value people first.** We are more than what happens during our office hours. We are human first and strive to show deep respect for every person inside and outside our company. We know that company culture matters, and we aspire to create an environment where our team can thrive as people and as professionals.

- **We value integrity and excellence.** We are honest, open, ethical, and fair. People trust us to adhere to our word, and we work hard to earn and maintain that trust. We always bring our best—to our work, our clients, and each other.

- **We value courageous leadership.** We act courageously and challenge the status quo; we find new ways to drive impact and equity to grow our company and each other.

- **We value strategic thinking and thoughtful execution.** We are not just seasoned consultants; we are experienced doers and collaborators. We understand the value of thoughtful analysis, clear rationale, and contextual communications in moving from ideas to implementation.

- **We value continuous learning and growth.** We are a dynamic team, continuously learning, innovating, and improving. We seek first to understand and apply what we learn to evolve and improve our work.

Our values reflect a triple-bottom-line philosophy driven by the positive and long-term effect our work can have on people and our planet rather than profit alone. And while you might presently see White at the top, I am proud of the women who lead our company and of the eyes-wide-open progress we're making to ensure the firm's long-term sustainability and shared ownership.

I've always known something deeper could be possible in our work. And communication, it seems, can be a very effective bridge between good intentions and greater impact.

It comes down to how we use what's in our power.

As my friend and colleague Natalie S. Burke says, "Power is the ability to define reality for yourself and others." Natalie is the President and CEO of CommonHealth ACTION and co-director of the Culture of Health Leaders program. She is a nationally recognized expert in health equity who has deeply informed my own work as a communications practitioner. Her words stay with me in the very best way because she says what so many are unwilling to accept.

Tremendous power exists in how we communicate our intentions and actions. Choosing your words is an important first step, but as we know, accomplishing long-term positive social change requires more than words. Communicating for change requires a commitment and willingness to explore, in-depth, what you *stand for*, how you *show up*, and how deep you're willing to *dig in*.

In the years since starting Mission Partners, we have worked with hundreds of organizations that are reckoning with the roles they've played—indirectly or directly—in contributing to harmful narratives or in the distance that exists between their board and their community's residents. We work with leaders who have lost the trust of their employees, and we support faith communities that want to do good without doing more harm. This doesn't mean we have it all figured out. I fail in this work, too. But I take my actions to heart and learn from those failures.

Communicating for change requires more than words; although the journey can be challenging, it can also be joyful.

The *practice*, as I've learned, is what matters.

In the coming chapters, I will highlight the practice we've built at Mission Partners, inspired by the four key communications practices of courageous leaders I've learned along my journey.

With stories from the field and guided prompts to help you explore how you show up in your work, this book will help you consider your own role in mission-moving work and the opportunity to deepen your impact.

Chapter 1

Truth

"The truth is not always beautiful,
nor beautiful words the truth."

LAO TZU

I am a recovering publicist.

OK, I've said it.

I spent the first two decades of my career working to amplify stories on behalf of hundreds of nonprofit organizations—mostly NGOs and social sector nonprofits—with good stories to tell but often without the resources to tell them. I have always been drawn to a good story, and I loved right from the start of my public relations career that on any given day, one good story could be amplified to reach millions of people. Talk about the potential for lasting change. Long before I graduated college, I was hooked. Public relations would be my path.

I landed my first public relations internship at sixteen, working for a small agency in northern New Jersey. I parlayed that position into a part-time job at a national magazine while in college before landing my first full-time job as

Director of Communications for Hall of Famer Cal Ripken, Jr., and his brother Bill Ripken, in support of their national Ripken Baseball initiative. The work was equally exhausting and exhilarating, and I learned I had a bit of a knack for storytelling and media relations. After supporting the Ripkens for a few years with their national baseball initiative and the launch of their Cal Ripken, Sr. Foundation, I moved to Washington, DC, to join a newly-established public affairs firm led by a team of highly respected communicators and DC insiders. It was inspiring, fast-paced, and a treasure trove of knowledge. I still consider my time at Prism Public Affairs among the most formative of my career.

At twenty-five, my soon-to-be husband and I moved to Hartford, Connecticut. He took on an exciting new role in marketing, and after a bit of a failed attempt to find a job that I loved as much as the one I held at Prism, I decided instead to see what I could do on my own. I opened the doors of C.Fox Communications in 2004, and over the next decade, grew it into a nationally recognized PR and communications firm supporting mission-driven organizations.

From the first story I landed and every story that followed throughout my PR career, I learned to savor the thrill of seeing my work in print or watching a story I had pitched unfold on the evening news. Better yet was to feel the ripples of those stories for the weeks that followed. Sometimes, my clients would receive five- and six-figure checks after a story had run; other times, they would be invited to the White House or to speak among some of the world's most sought-after funders. And in the best of instances, my work would lead to new federal policies or laws designed to improve the human condition.

There was something truly mission-moving in telling a good story.

And so, I got to work and honed my craft. I watched, learned, and took every opportunity I could find to dig into the world of nonprofit communications and purpose-driven PR.

From that first agency job at sixteen and through every job that followed, my instinct was to find and promote stories that could help nonprofit organizations and charities raise more money. I learned how to position stories that journalists couldn't resist by providing them with behind-the-scenes access to all the data, all the angles, and all the resources to tell a great, emotional, and sticky story.

But as I came to learn in 2016, my style of communications was working on the surface, and also holding organizations back.

I needed a new way and a wider lens.

The Backstory

My worldview as a child was formed through the lens fashioned by my immediate and extended family. As the great-grandchild of Italian immigrants who settled in northern New Jersey after arriving in Ellis Island, I learned culture, history, politics, and religion through a whitewashed lens of stories, history, and experiences of my youth. I had White dolls, White teachers, and White main characters in my storybooks. We celebrated Christopher Columbus with a parade and a statue in front of the local library. We learned only bits of America's full story and even less about the failings of that story. I was aware enough to feel something was not quite right, but as a child, I was not confident enough to challenge it. I took what I learned throughout childhood as truth because the people around me told me it was true.

I left my predominantly White community in New Jersey for a predominantly White college in Baltimore. I was learning amid great privilege while mere steps from immense poverty. As a student, I co-existed in this heartbreaking environment, knowing something was terribly wrong, but I did not yet have the courage or skills to do something about it. Little did I know how connected this part of my journey would be to my future.

I opened the doors to my first company, C.Fox Communications in 2004, shortly after my twenty-fifth birthday. As I slowly built the company, I felt good about supporting non-profit organizations by amplifying their feel-good stories. I was happy to be making it as a small business owner. I provided pro bono services to worthy causes and secured front-page coverage that resulted in high-value donations. But still, something was fundamentally wrong. I supported dozens of social service organizations through storytelling and fundraising but never once challenged whether their models worked. I never considered if we were telling the full story or just bits of it. I never questioned if we were doing more harm than good.

Along the way, I had the opportunity to work with and learn from a man named Mauricio Lim Miller. He didn't look like me. He didn't think like me. But he believed in me. And I loved him for it.

By the time I met him, Mauricio had become recognized internationally for his work in challenging foundational concepts such as the American Dream. He rebutted the idea that hard work leads to economic success. In the social services sector where he worked, plenty of hardworking families were seemingly stuck in a rotating door of safety net support without access to the resources they truly needed to achieve economic mobility. No matter how hard they worked, they did not achieve economic stability. Mauricio knew the system was broken, not the people within it.

For context, Mauricio is the son of a hardworking single mother who left Mexico in the 1950s to escape domestic abuse and find a better life for her young children. A talented dressmaker, she left her own life behind to ensure that her children had access to education and systems that would support their lifelong prosperity. Mauricio had access to education and made it to the University of California, Berkeley, where he studied engineering before moving into social services. He worked in the exact type of social service programs he had seen trying to help his mother in those early years in a new country. But it wasn't long before Mauricio realized that the social supports people received—in the form of temporary shelter, tenant rights, job training, or access to basic educational services—weren't helping much at all. They weren't moving people from one place in life to another. Instead, these services provided a rotating door, keeping people stuck in a system and preventing them from moving themselves or their families forward.

Mauricio's a-ha was that the federal government had created a flawed social services system whose failings were then reinforced by local governments, nonprofits, and foundations. Everyone responsible for maintaining this flawed system became part of the problem, but most were too close to recognize the harm it inflicted on society, communities, and families like his. He envisioned an alternative. He believed that by investing in the initiative of families—rather than propping up more programs—people could chart their own paths to success, and poverty numbers might decline as a result.

In 2012, Miller was honored as a MacArthur Genius grant winner[3] for the simple yet breakthrough approach of his Family Independence Initiative (FII). Mauricio's alternative to the social service model fostered an atmosphere that was part idea incubator and part learning laboratory. Rather than serve as helpers or solutions-providers to families, FII employees shifted the responsibility for setting goals, finding solutions, and initiating action to participating members themselves. Families receive small cash stipends for achieving their self-initiated goals—such as finding employment, reducing debt, or saving toward buying a home—and for documenting and sharing their progress toward these goals.[4]

Over ten years of a pilot program, Mauricio and his team proved unequivocally that choice, capital, and community are the key factors in moving people out of poverty into sustainable and lasting economic mobility. Rather than reinforce what was broken about the system, he leaned on the power of peer-to-peer encouragement and social networking. His work counteracted the thousands of private and public anti-poverty initiatives meant to do good but often did harm—the kinds of programs I was promoting.

In all my years working on issues of poverty alleviation, the Family Independence Initiative remains the most successful and honest approach I've ever seen.

Through my work with Mauricio and with projects in the foster care system and community-based nonprofits around the country, many of which I'll introduce you to in the coming chapters, I began deepening my understanding of the role that individual people—you and me—play in shaping, sharing, and reinforcing stories that directly influence how we understand the world around us. I began seeing how individual people *can* affect change in their communities and how individual people *can* move visions for a more just world forward.

How we communicate is one of the greatest levers for change. It comes down to how we use the power we have.

For instance, the stories we tell sometimes influence great outcomes: they make us see and believe what we're capable of and inspire us to act. But other times, stories—like some of those from my childhood, or those Mauricio saw in the social services sector, or the story I shared in the introduction of this book—reinforce false or harmful narratives that limit social progress from taking hold.

Courageous leadership requires courageous communication. And while the journey may last a lifetime, you're exactly where you need to be to get started.

BOTTOM LINE: The stories we've been told about who succeeds, who doesn't, and why limit our ability to see broken systems when we come across them. Communication is a critical factor. We must see, understand, acknowledge, and then take action when something is not working as intended. If we can't see it, feel it, or understand it, we can't expect to be able to do anything meaningful about it.

Chapter 2

Design in Everything We Do

"Design is the intention
(and unintentional impact)
behind an outcome."

ANTOINETTE CARROLL

I am a White, cis-gender Christian woman of Italian heritage, college educated, over forty, and able-bodied. I have unearned privilege, advantage, and power. As a small business owner, and in line with our company's commitments as a Certified Benefit Corporation, I do my best to use that position of power to disrupt many of the dominant cultural norms that had been, by default, instilled in me. I don't always get it right, but as I hope you'll find through this book, so much of how we show up is in our willingness to learn, understand, and celebrate what makes each of us authentic rather than celebrate what makes us perfect.

From my time working alongside Mauricio and the hundreds of other social change leaders I've supported in these past decades, I've noticed that the most effective leaders embody an ever-present core set of elements in their leadership style. These aspects, without fail, lead to some organizations being highly effective in their ability to acknowledge, disrupt, and improve systems, compared to other leaders who tend to keep the systems at the status quo.

In the best-case scenarios, I consider these effective leaders to be *communicators for change*. They take to heart the influence that media, messages, and marketing can have on people. They use their platforms to acknowledge systemic and personal failures and are grounded in their values and in service of more just and equitable outcomes. They understand that design is in everything we do, whether designer is in our title or not. The systems we design, the programs we design, and the communications campaign we design all have an effect. Therefore, the communicator for change inherently understands the power and responsibility of that design and the need for those designs to be inclusive, equitable, and thoughtful in their approach.

In the following chapters, those characteristics are broken down even more. You'll find prompts to explore your own role as a communicator and suggestions for improving your effectiveness as a communicator for change.

So, let's get to it.

Chapter 3

Power Skills

"You've always had the power...
you had to learn it for yourself."

GLINDA THE GOOD IN THE WIZARD OF OZ

For the past twenty years, I have used communication as my primary tool to change and improve systems. But I didn't understand how deeply connected leadership communication was to organizational success until more recently. With experience, I reflected back and realized that in every one of the hundreds of organizations I've worked with over twenty years, as well as in the hundreds of organizations I've studied over the same time, one factor determined an organization's ability to use communications as an effective power tool for social change: the human factor.

Let's look at this a little closer.

Not long ago, I worked with an executive who believed her team didn't need her anymore. She deeply wanted to engage her colleagues in critical conversations on diversity, equity, inclusion, and belonging, but she felt uncomfortable leading conversations without being an expert on the issues.

She doubted her ability to lead the work, which led to her team doubting her too.

Over time she retreated until she reached her a-ha moment. Through our work together, she realized she'd never get the engagement she wanted from her team, nor any real shot at disrupting the inequitable systems their organization was working to upend, until she changed how *she engaged* as a leader—openly, honestly, and *without* all the answers.

Once her mindset shifted, so too did her communications style. She became more candid and less controlled. She started to see that how she communicated directly affected the resulting work. Trust was deepened, the team began to flourish, and the outcomes became more meaningful.

The changes were slight, but the result was transformational.

I could tell this story hundreds of times over about leaders—me included—who doubt their effectiveness in mission-critical moments and how their organizations struggle as a result. But never have I seen this issue as pronounced as I see it in today's work environment.

According to a recent Catalyst study[5], nine out of ten people feel emotionally or physically unsafe to speak their minds in the workplace. Issues of identity, belonging, equity, and inclusion are paramount in all workforces. But according to our own recent research,[6] very few executives feel equipped with the communications skills required to lead their teams effectively through this time. That disconnect in communications skills is causing unnecessary breakdowns, misunderstandings, and lost opportunities for all involved.

What if, instead, leaders fostered spaces where people trusted themselves and one another to communicate honestly and openly, without all the answers, but with a commitment to learn and grow together? To "get comfortable with the uncomfortable," as Natalie Burke says, in service of something bigger than any one of us. It's easier said than done, but I also believe it is imperative for any team or organization looking to achieve its greatest transformational impact.

So, that brings us to this book and my belief that communication can be one of the greatest levers for change. It's a tool for trust-building and trust-keeping. It's also far more of a power skill than many people care to believe. Too many people leave their most important communication in the hands of experts to figure out, limiting the change-making power that they can have.

Systems Won't Change
Unless People Do

To understand the wide-reaching relevance of communication as a tool for social change, let's zoom in on a different set of powers—those created by Marvel Entertainment.

In 2020, the video game world learned that Marvel's latest Spider-Man character, Miles Morales—the Latino and African-American teenager who replaced Marvel's iconic Peter Parker—was skilled in American Sign Language (ASL). This version of the fictional superhero was already known to be bilingual, but ASL was a newly-introduced trait, making Morales the first known trilingual superhero.

That trait opened even more doors for Marvel Entertainment, who soon after introduced another character named Hailey Cooper, a Black deaf street artist and community organizer. Hailey Cooper is played by a Black deaf female actress named Natasha Ofili, who has said that she didn't have anyone growing up that represented her on television, let alone in video games.

Learning about Spider-Man's new sign language skills and this important new character in the Spider-Man story made me wonder: was this a new trait, or had some sign been there from the start?

After digging in, I found that one essential ASL gesture has indeed always been part of Spider-Man's powers, and The Library of Congress can prove it. Spider-Man's specific hand gesture happens to be the very same ASL sign for love.

For so long, I just hadn't noticed.

Stan Lee, the creator of the original webbed superhero, once said that he picked that finger pose for Spider-Man because of its meaning, and he wanted Spider-Man to apprehend criminals with love.

What started as one sign became a call to action for the Marvel enterprise of today to lean into a much more inclusive version of its young action hero and an opportunity to represent the Black deaf community in mainstream media in a way that had never been done before. Not too different, really, from Mauricio's sign to reimagine a social services sector or my earlier example of a nonprofit executive's sign to let some of her vulnerability show.

All three of these initial stories spark something vital that we'll cover many times through this book and are best summed up in the words of Dr. Maya Angelou, "Do the best you can until you know better. Then, when you know better, do better."

> ## "Do the best you can until you know better. Then, when you know better, do better."
>
> DR. MAYA ANGELOU

Given the current state of our workplaces, society, and democracy, I believe the time to do better has been here for some time. And the *power* to do better is in each of our hands. How we engage on difficult topics or in divisive moments comes down to how we view and value communications and, more importantly, how we view and value each other. We need bridges to communicate now more than ever, particularly if we're in this for systems-changing results.

You can be that bridge.

In its July–August 2022 issue,[7] *Harvard Business Review* released findings of a study that noted inclusive leadership as among the most essential traits for today's C-Suite leaders. More important than technical prowess, superior administrative skills, or a track record of effective management are people skills—specifically, interpersonal communications skills. But, as you might imagine, having the skills isn't enough; how you choose to prioritize them in your daily work and actions is the crucial point.

Just as Marvel noticed a sign and reimagined a character, or as Mauricio Miller's picked at a system and reimagined an alternative, the power is in each of us to reimagine the outcome.

Could you do the same in your work?

In the following chapters, we'll explore more examples like this in-depth to help you uncover your own opportunities for greater impact, including:

- A national campaign advocating for improvements to the U.S. foster care system. The campaign's executive moved out of the way in crucial moments and supported the voice of youth and lived experience. The result was sweeping policy change, directly informed by young people who had experienced the system's failings first-hand.

- A one-hundred-year-old organization that realized how it was telling its story had unintended consequences on the outcomes of its community. By changing the frame, they also changed the trajectory of their work.

- A global, multi-million-dollar contest to advance planet-friendly alternatives to gasoline. The contest's leadership team recognized the role that an unlikely group of teens from West Philadelphia, Pennsylvania, could play in breaking America's addiction to oil.

- One of the world's most successful tech companies whose executive chose to see talent in everyone, including in the unlikeliest places. It then built a powerful blueprint for hiring talent, influencing an entire sector of IT hiring managers.

In each of these examples, and others shared throughout the book, a set of essential characteristics appear. Together those qualities reflect the four practices of courageous leaders and communicators for change:

1. **The First Practice: Dare to Ask.** A leader—whether an executive, board member, or team manager—is willing to challenge and change a norm. Rather than defaulting to the expected spokesperson or communications strategy, courageous leaders see the opportunity to tell a story from a different lens.

2. **The Second Practice: Dig Down to the Roots.** Rather than communicating superficially, courageous leaders are willing to look and look again at the issues in front of them. They are ready to disrupt and challenge dominant norms and patterns to elicit true social change.

3. **The Third Practice: See Your Story as Bigger Than the Moment.** The leaders presented in this book are truly leaders of movements, not of moments. They rely on a wide lens to understand the world around them and their place in it. Courageous leaders realize the power of their words and actions to move people, organizations, and issues forward. They aren't in it for short-term gain but rather the long-term impact.

4. **The Fourth Practice: Follow Through.** The examples in this book are not one-and-done strategies. They are ways of living and showing up in service to the world that require continuous commitment and care. To become a courageous leader and effective social change communicator, you, too, must develop your practice and follow through, over and over and over again.

In each of these examples, just as in the opening stories about Mauricio Miller, Marvel Entertainment, and our well-intentioned nonprofit executive, the signs for social change were always present because of the people and teams leading the change. The signs were always there. And I believe the signs for social change and transformative impact are present in your work, too. It's up to you whether or not you choose to see and act on them.

> **BOTTOM LINE:** How, where, and when we communicate plays a big part in our ability to move our teams, work, and missions forward. If any part of your mission intersects with a desire to build more just and equitable systems, this book can help.

Chapter 4

What's At Stake

"If we cared about equity, we would
have done something about it already."

DR. MICHAEL SORRELL

As leaders and managers, most of us know exactly what's at stake when running an effective organization. But many of us still feel ill-equipped to communicate effortlessly through these moments as expected.

According to a recent survey[8], 68 percent of employees believe their organization's COVID-related policies for the care and safety of their workers were not genuine. In White-majority countries, three-quarters of employees also reported that their organization's racial equity policies were not genuine.

If you're caught up in the words, connecting genuinely can feel even more daunting.

Ilya Pozin offered a bit of explanation in *Forbes*,[9] "In an era when personal identities are complicated by nuanced expressions of gender, race, religion, nationality, language, and so much more, brands are attempting to become even more sensitive, and connect authentically with consumers who are skeptical of what is typically a predominantly White marketing landscape."

But connecting authentically can feel pretty overwhelming when you're struggling to figure out what to do and how to say it.

"The ability to listen, relate, and understand what employees are experiencing—that has separated good leaders from great ones during the pandemic, and may hold the key to keeping employees engaged during what's been termed the Great Resignation," said the authors of the Catalyst survey.

According to the same survey, a key determinant in whether employees perceived COVID-related and racial equity policies positively was the very same factor—leader empathy. Leaders who used their empathy skills were better able to create and communicate an authentic, equitable vision for the future and reap the employee and organizational benefits.

Dr. Michael Sorrell, President of Paul Quinn College, said in a 2020 webinar about the state of higher education in America, "If we cared about equity, we would have done something about it already." While the reference is about one sector, it's also a universal statement that I've never been able to forget. If our workplaces cared, if our local governments cared, if our faith communities cared.

> The mission of Paul Quinn College is to provide a quality, faith-based education that addresses the academic, social, and Christian development of students and prepares them to be servant leaders and agents of change in the global marketplace. It is a powerful and explicit mission, one that they deliver effectively.

I believe leaders do care about equity. But for many leaders, getting to a place where they feel ready and willing to do what the world needs from them—to act in service of the public good without getting sidelined by profit—is easier said than done.

Understanding the values we hold within our organization is an essential step toward implementing the long-term change that Mauricio enacted. Do you regularly practice care for all people, or do you show a preference for certain identities, work habits, or character traits? If so, why?

These are important questions to ask and to dig into.

THINK ABOUT THIS. What parts of your history inform how you show up as a communicator and a leader? What have you carried forward, for better or worse, that shows up in your daily words and actions?

WRITE THIS DOWN. Jot down a few memories from early career experiences that have stayed with you. How do they make you feel now, given the space of time?

As you set out on this journey, remember this: you don't need to have all the answers, and you don't need to get all the words just right. But once we know better, we can do better.

Part 1

Communication Practices of Courageous Leaders

Dare to Ask

"To dare is to lose one's
footing momentarily.
Not to dare is to lose oneself."

SOREN KIERKEGAARD

Have you ever thought, as you see something unnerving, inappropriate, or downright harmful playing out at work, in a community meeting, or even among friends or neighbors, *I should really say something.*

Maybe a different perspective could be useful at the moment, or additional context might help steer the conversation. Maybe an intervention could help right the wrong. But instead, you choose not to say anything. You doubt yourself. You don't want to cause a scene or distract from the conversation at hand.

You don't want to upset someone. You don't think it's worth it. You don't even know what to say.

You feel the urge *to say something* but stop short because you don't know what to say or feel comfortable saying it.

But *what if.*

What if you had the words, the confidence, and the readiness to communicate in those moments?

Putting yourself in a position to ask *what if* does not require sharing your position or having a point of view. Being willing to ask *what if* is an open door to examine a situation from a new perspective and to let others know what's on your mind. Asking *what if* isn't always about finding the answer or scolding someone for their approach. It's first about sparking a conversation. And conversation can lead to greater understanding, which can lead to positive change.

As you contemplate the first practice, consider these questions, and then revisit your answers after reading the book:

THINK ABOUT THIS. Are you developing communications that reinforce false or negative stereotypes, or are you helping to reshape narratives in a way that diffuses those stereotypes?

WRITE THIS DOWN. Think of one norm that you maintain in your communications style. *What if* you challenged, questioned, or changed that norm by radically listening? Document what you learn and consider what you can change as a result. Then ask again and again, *what if?*

Chapter 5

What If?

"At first glance, it may appear too hard.
Look again. Always look again."

MARY ANNE RADMACHER

A friend of mine is an advertising executive responsible for art directing several well-known and well-loved consumer campaigns. Over the past two decades, his work has moved millions of people to action in support of dozens of brands and causes.

In a recent conversation, we discussed the power of communications and the role that communicators—in big agencies and small—can play in shaping opinions, perceptions, and movements. Our decisions as creative directors can either break stereotypes or reinforce them. They can challenge narratives or perpetuate them.

As we talked, it became abundantly clear that two little words have the power to change *how* we communicate and *how* we connect with and understand one another as a result.

Those two words? You guessed it. *What if?*

What if we—the global community of communicators, marketers, and designers—took every available opportunity to shift how messages are told? *What if* we took every opportunity to explore the standards and norms that exist in our communications and then shifted those norms to inform even more inclusive, accessible, and equitable messages? And what might be the long-term effect on our communities, society, and the world?

I have long believed that communication is the greatest tool to advance social justice. I have seen time and again what is truly possible when we dare to ask *what if* and then lean into imagining and asking what's possible through clear, focused, and effective communication.

Here are some ways I've seen this work remarkably well:

- A public health communicator wants to change the face of public health in the U.S. and launches a 40 Under 40 list to celebrate an entire generation of innovators, entrepreneurs, and equity champions who are influencing the field but who had previously not been seen or celebrated as leaders.

- A centuries-old nonprofit celebrates the power of young changemakers by shifting away from the long-established spokesperson to a vibrant team of young people who show the power of this brand in action.

- And one of the biggest consumer brands in the world uses its platform to show the real experiences of women navigating postpartum, showing what a brand *can do* with its platform to widen the lens on a critical issue.

BOTTOM LINE: Whether you manage a big brand or a small startup, a team of thousands or a team of two, power is inherent in every single one of your communications decisions, power to shift and shape narratives for good.

Dare to ask, *what if*, and I guarantee the answer will inspire you.

Chapter 6

Listening Skills

"Change happens by listening and then starting a dialogue with the people who are doing something you don't believe is right."

JANE GOODALL

Shortly after the COVID-19 pandemic began, I was on a call with a group of foundation presidents discussing ways to communicate a public health message to their broad set of constituents. The conversation started as you might expect, with various ideas being shared, followed by a discussion to explore some of the stickier ideas. And then, one of the presidents popped in and emphatically recommended, "I process information best visually, so I think we should really prioritize visuals in this message."

Sure, on the surface, his idea of delivering a visual message was a good one. Multimedia content is known to be more engaging across cultures and platforms. But it was *how* he made the recommendation that stuck with me. In this case, the video was the solution that felt most natural and compelling for *him*, someone who did not represent the audience or have any shared lived experiences with them. He was adamant that this solution was the best solution.

This little exchange stuck with me as a reminder of how quickly we make recommendations for improving communication without ever getting close to the subject.

When We Know Better, We Do Better

It's natural to share an idea or move the team in a direction that most comfortably aligns with your experiences. The important distinction as a communicator for change is knowing the difference between offering ideas that work for you and offering ideas that meet your audience where they are.

How might this audience have preferred to receive the message? In what language? On what platform? Too often, I hear, "We don't have the resources to do that kind of research, so we're going to do the best we can."

The reality is most of us are just too far from the main characters in the story we're trying to tell even to know the answer.

I'm sure you can relate. Pause here for a moment and think of a time when you felt yourself holding back from a conversation in which you want to be more engaged. Now, consider *what if*:

- *What if* you reached out to a few colleagues to explore individual or small group conversations on key topics rather than diving into a large group conversation?

- *What if* you led a listening session with a few interested colleagues rather than facilitating a large group discussion?

- *What if* you didn't wait until you had all the answers but explored those answers together with your colleagues?

What change might start to take hold as a result? Take the time to listen. It will always be worth it.

Learning to Listen

In nonprofit and philanthropy sectors, calls have increased in intensity for funders and organizational leaders to listen more closely and engage more authentically with community members with the greatest stake in community-level decisions. Who knows better, of course, than residents of a given community about how a change in that community will be received? And who better to help solve community-level challenges than the residents directly impacted by those challenges? Sounds simple enough, but that doesn't mean it is done universally well.

Most efforts, as Mauricio Miller notes, are "...half-hearted attempts that do not actually let participants lead their own change... It is time to give up power and instead facilitate and resource the efforts of everyday people."

As Mauricio found in social service programming, residents already lead some of the best efforts in creating businesses, jobs, and projects that improve the community for everyone. Those efforts go unrecognized. Instead, nonprofit and government efforts get attention and money. Most self-organized efforts do not need an NGO to inspire or lead them. If we want change, those seeking to change things must support these self-help efforts.

Whether you want to hear it or not, the same is true in communications. Those of us holding the pens shouldn't assume we know the best way to tell a story or to communicate an issue. Inspired by Mauricio's work, we call this process "radical listening."

Radical listening is a process that can build trust and strengthen relationships. It takes basic listening—and even active listening—a step further.

Building Empathy Through Radical Listening

Test your own skills as a radical listener. For this activity, find a partner, preferably a colleague, an acquaintance, a friend, or a neighbor. Face one another. For sixty seconds, gaze into each other's eyes without speaking or laughing. Don't break eye contact!

Reflect on how this felt—for you and your partner.

Next, one person will speak for sixty seconds on any topic. The other person will listen without interrupting or saying anything. Keep eye contact with one another throughout this process. After sixty seconds, switch roles—the listener will now speak, and the speaker will now listen. Then, reflect on how this felt for you and your partner.

For several minutes, have a dialogue discussing what you both heard previously. Then discuss.

- How did that process feel? What emotions emerged?

- What connections or commonalities have emerged between you and your partner?

- What was the point of this activity?

- How might this conversation have been different without radical listening?

- How often do you listen to your community in this way?

This type of radical listening isn't new, but it is essential to build an empathetic mindset and bridge gaps in understanding that are often the barriers to social change.

Radical Listening Supports Radical Empathy

Denise Villa and Jason Dorsey examined the importance of empathetic listening in their book, *ZConomy*. They found that Generation Z does not process and receive information the same way Generation X or baby boomers will. Generationally, culturally, and geographically, we hear and process information differently. So, rather than default to communicating in culturally dominant or generation-specific ways, consider how you could alter or change your tone, platform, cadence, and even spokesperson to connect with your stakeholders more effectively and authentically.

The best place to start? You guessed it—listening. We all want to be heard. Being heard is essential to building a relationship based on trust. So, make a practice of actively and radically listening to the words and in between the words. It will help you become an even better communicator.

Active, deep, and radical listening is where good and effective communicators begin. You might first understand who you are talking with, how they prefer to process information, and what they need to hear if you expect them to hear you, trust you, and take your intended action. Start by listening if you wish to move people to action.

More Tips for Radical Listening:

ACTIVELY FOCUS. Make and maintain eye contact.

WATCH YOUR SIGNALS. Set distractions aside so you can remain open, patient, and immersed in the conversation.

PRACTICE PAUSING. Avoid jumping to conclusions, making assumptions or judgments, or speaking over people's words; everyone speaks once before anyone speaks twice.

STOP SELLING. After sharing ideas, just listen; let your mind absorb what it's hearing rather than drive towards what you want to say next.

CONFIRM YOU HEARD CORRECTLY. Summarize what you heard back to the speaker.

From Comics to Coding:
Slack's Big *What If* Moment

Getting to a place where we can effect positive social change through our communications starts with listening carefully and asking *what if*, just like Marvel Entertainment did as they worked to build an authentically evolved and more inclusive Spider-Man.

To help us explore this practice more closely, let's take a look at Slack, the billion-dollar unicorn company founded by Stewart Butterfield in 2009 and purchased by Salesforce in 2021.

But first, let's head back to the Slack of 2015.

After reading Bryan Stevenson's book *Just Mercy*, Slack CEO Stewart Butterfield felt an urgent need to address the inequities of America's criminal justice system. The Canadian businessman had long believed that while "talent might be evenly distributed in the world, opportunity is not," as he told me in a 2019 interview documenting this work. He wanted to explore what would happen if a large technology company launched an intentional technology-training program for incarcerated people as one way to shift how and where opportunities are distributed.

So, in 2016, Butterfield and a small group of his senior team visited San Quentin prison, twenty miles north of San Francisco. There, he met Aly Tamboura, who was at that time a student of The Last Mile program, which provides education and training inside prison. The program has been proven to reduce recidivism by providing access to gainful employment for returned citizen graduates.[10] Butterfield was so impressed with Aly that he directed his team at Slack to start an informal partnership with The Last Mile to explore how they might hire Aly when he was released.

Here was the situation when the exploration began:[11]

- Ninety-five percent of incarcerated individuals return home and re-enter their communities. But because of the stigma associated with a criminal conviction, the unemployment rate is nearly five times as high for formerly incarcerated individuals than that of the general U.S. population.

- Research shows that a lack of stable employment drastically increases the likelihood of an individual returning to jail or prison—making joblessness a leading predictor of recidivism.

- This counterproductive cycle of release and poverty hurts everyone—including reentering individuals, employers, and taxpayers.

Slack's leadership knew the problem was bigger than any one company could take on alone, but they also knew the inequities had persisted for too long. They believed they could play a role in changing the outcome. They just needed to figure out how.

And so, upon Aly's completion of The Last Mile program, Slack sponsored Aly to attend a prestigious coding boot camp and invited him through the standard hiring process. Though Aly graduated from The Last Mile program, he couldn't pass Slack's interview process and instead accepted a job elsewhere that allowed him to pursue a career in social justice.

Slack's leadership still views the inability to hire Aly as an early failure in the process. "We wanted badly to hire Aly but couldn't ignore the skills gap that existed between what he had learned at the boot camp he attended and what he needed to know to be a Slack engineer," said Deepti Rohatgi, Executive Director of Slack for Good.

This failure gave the Slack team the drive and energy to do something—to design a better partnership that would work for Slack as much as it would work for those graduating from The Last Mile. It could mean continuously asking *what if*, listening deeply, and being willing to try things that had never been done before. It would also require continuous and transparent communications by leadership about the process to their employees and stakeholders.

"It took a C-Suite leader to make a program like Next Chapter a priority," added Rohatgi. "Given the cross-functional support that was needed for this program to be successful, it was critical to have the leadership team on board—and to have them communicate their commitment to this effort every step of the way."

Daring to ask *what if*, listening closely to those most affected by the injustice, and following through openly and honestly in their commitment led to an even more thoughtful program with far greater outcomes.

Today, Slack has hired nine Next Chapter apprentices as full-time employees. Nearly fifty apprentices have graduated from the program and received full-time job offers across fourteen participating hiring companies.

Slack committed to this program for the long-term because it knew re-entry programs could improve outcomes for returning individuals. They also know that comprehensive reentry programs give tech companies unique opportunities to offer meaningful career opportunities—building their talent pipelines and reducing recidivism. But to be most effective, they couldn't do it alone. Their Blueprint for Change,[12] which my team and I helped develop, has now been used by dozens of tech companies in Silicon Valley and beyond, multiplying the effect of their work.

BOTTOM LINE: As leaders and communicators, we have a responsibility to listen—carefully and intentionally. It's our job to get close to the audience and to act when we see injustice at work. And one of the best ways to do that is to start by asking, "*What if?*"

Chapter 7

What's Hiding in Your Communications?

"Normal led to this."

ED YONG

Ed Yong is a Pulitzer Prize-winning science writer at *The Atlantic* who served as a constant source of insight and wisdom during the COVID-19 pandemic. But before his award-winning pandemic reporting, Yong spent two years trying to fix a gender imbalance he discovered in his stories.

Inspired by his colleague Adrienne LaFrance, who conducted a similar assessment across all *Atlantic* journalism, he found that only 24 percent of his last twenty-three articles quoted women sources. And of those stories, 35 percent featured no female voices at all.

Here's what he said in reflecting on his findings:

"I knew that I cared about equality, so I deluded myself into thinking that I wasn't part of the problem. I assumed that my passive concern would be enough. Passive concern never is."

Yong's heartbreakingly honest revelation spurred my desire to dig in on ways that writers, marketers, and communications directors can build equity and break bias in their storytelling. From NPR to *National Geographic*, major news organizations have started looking inward to reduce their long-held reporting biases. That same fervor to address implicit bias in storytelling isn't yet showing up in the same way from communications directors, marketing directors, and content producers of non-media organizations—even though it should.

Ed's story, and others like it, reinforced for me that as communicators, we inherently believe that we're telling our best stories. It's easy to think we're telling our best stories, but the reality of implicit bias is that we bring it to the table without realizing it.

How much bias would you uncover if you assessed the stories on your own website, in your most recent annual report, or across your marketing campaigns? *What if* the stories you've been telling are actually *limiting* your ability to communicate with your most important audiences? *What if*, in elevating your organization's "best" stories, you unintentionally leave out some of the most vital voices from your organization's narrative?

Biases exist in all of us based on our own lived experiences. But anyone can learn to break biases in storytelling with the right tools and perspective.

When you focus on who your stories are about and who benefits from them, you're more likely to be inclusive in your storytelling. Bias-free language does not discriminate but instead includes all readers in a fair and friendly manner.

Assess your own unconscious attitudes and associations to better inform your storytelling. One of the most effective and free tools for testing your own unconscious bias is the Implicit Association Test (IAT), created and maintained by Project Implicit, a consortium comprised of researchers from Harvard University, the University of Virginia, and the University of Washington.

Inspired in part by the findings of Ed Yong and other journalists, here are a few tips we've developed to help organizations communicate through an equity lens:

- Review your writing for the **appropriate use of pronouns** to ensure neutrality when referring to a person's gender identity. For instance, "each manager must report his numbers at the end of the month" presents a bias, compared to "all managers must report their numbers at the end of the month." Replace gender-biased terms, such as salesman, chairman or congresswoman, with bias-free terms, such as salesperson, chairperson, or member of congress. For a deeper dive into the use of gender-neutral pronouns, including the use of non-binary pronouns, check out the *New York Times* article by Raillan Brooks.[13]

- Focus on people, not their conditions or current state. In other words, **use person-first and/or identity-first language**. We all experience challenges in our lives, but one need not be defined by those challenges. Notice the difference between describing a homeless person and a person experiencing homelessness or a foster youth versus a young person living in foster care.

- **Be mindful of euphemisms that reinforce ableism.** Using a phrase such as *blind spot* to describe a lack of knowledge or willful ignorance—such as "the senator has a blind spot on certain issues"—is not respectful of people who are blind as it references a visual impairment to describe a lack of knowledge.

Here are a few more euphemisms to consider swapping out of your vocabulary, with credit to IndieSpace.org for their insightful article[14] on the topic:

- **Crazy:** Many people use phrases like "That's so crazy!" or "They were acting insane." These words can be stigmatizing for people with lived experiences of mental health conditions. Many individuals have shared their reluctance, fear, and anxiety in seeking mental health support because they may be labeled by friends, colleagues, or loved ones as crazy or insane.

- **Lame:** This word is often used to describe something or a situation that is bad, frustrating, or dull. However, many don't know—or remember—that the definition of this word is to have a body part, often a limb, so injured that it impairs freedom of movement. Better word choices are available that don't use historical references that may harm your audience.

Just because a phrase is commonly used does not mean it is inclusive to all members of your community.

Make content accessible.

Beyond examining who is showing up in photos and which voices are being elevated, consider localizing your content, so it is most accessible within your community. That could mean translating your content into the local languages or developing a closed-captioned version of your organizational video. Take the time to ensure that everyone in your community can access and understand the messages you're sending.

Your organization's most important and influential voices are not always the most expected.

For years, organizations have been pressed to present their value via stories, often elevating one or two of the best examples. This small set of success stories is rarely representative of the whole. It may reinforce your organization's biases by portraying what your organization believes is a picture of success versus what your community might believe to be a success.

Before publishing your next article, annual report, or research brief, check your work with a fresh set of eyes, and always make time for community feedback. Ask what changes they'd make to strengthen the story and make it more inclusive. You can also ask yourself:

- Are the pronouns she, he, and they used close to an equal number of times?

- Is any language about people written as people-first, as in people with diabetes instead of diabetics?

- Have labels or conditions been misused as nouns to describe a group, for example, the city's homeless population?

- Do you know, or do you need to ask, which term is preferred for a national origin, race, or gender identification for a specific audience?

BOTTOM LINE: It often takes an outside perspective to help discover an unconscious bias. Make time at the start of your writing process for community input, and you'll have a much better, more informed, and more accurate article in the end.

THE SECOND PRACTICE

Dig In

"The past can hurt. But the way I see it,
you can either run from it or learn from it."

WALT DISNEY

I often say that the day I stop learning will be the day I walk away from my business. I consider it a core part of my responsibility as a business owner and consultant to fellow leaders to be learning, evolving, and challenging myself to grow, particularly in the places where I feel discomfort, as that always unlocks the greatest work for my company and for my clients. As mentioned in Chapter 3, Natalie Burke calls it "getting comfortable with the uncomfortable," and I wholeheartedly agree with its benefit for those seeking to be social change communicators.

As I reflect on my years as a small business owner, as the founder of a purpose-driven B Corporation, and as a parent, I've realized that this *learning, unlearning, and learning new* is the best way to stay connected to my craft, and to the people with whom I work, while staying invigorated in the business.

- I've learned that understanding a system's design is essential before attempting to disrupt it.

- I've learned to appreciate the wonder in a story's roots and not to take for granted the role that history plays in working toward future change.

- And as noted above, I've learned to lean into discomfort as an essential practice to understand where inequities persist and to dismantle harm through my action rather than perpetuate them through uninformed communications.

In this second practice, we will explore what it means to really dig into our communications. We'll learn to take note of communications when they're happening on autopilot and to reimagine communications practices that might be holding you back. To do that, we'll introduce you to leaders who understand the value of digging in. Rather than communicating superficially, you'll learn from leaders willing to disrupt and challenge dominant norms and patterns for the sake of true social change.

Here are a few guiding questions to consider while reading the next pages:

THINK ABOUT THIS. What do you do on autopilot? What communications approaches have become too comfortable? What templates have started to feel a little tired? Building on experience is good, but if you stop learning, it is bound to show.

WRITE THIS DOWN. What is one communication process that you're ready to refresh? What power and/or privilege do you hold over the community affected by the project?

Chapter 8

Get Closer

"If we begin to teach history exactly the way that it happened—good, bad, ugly, no matter what—we're going to find that we are closer, more connected than we are apart."

RUBY BRIDGES

When engineers set out to design the first Apple mouse, they weren't sure which design would be best—the design that had one mouse button or two. Before moving forward, they had to figure out what kind of mouse they wanted to build and, more importantly, what they were solving for.

That was in the early 1980s, and the process used by those Apple engineers formed the start of a process now widely known as design thinking.

"Before you do problem-solving, you have to do problem-finding," said Dave Evans, a former Apple engineer who worked on the Apple mouse project and then co-founded the game company Electronic Arts.

WHAT IS DESIGN THINKING?

Design thinking is a human-centered process for solving problems by prioritizing the consumer's needs above all else. It relies on observing, with deep empathy, how people interact with their environments. It employs an iterative, hands-on approach to creating new problem-solving strategies rather than leaning on existing solutions. The design thinking methodology was first popularized by design consulting firm IDEO, www.ideo.com, whose founder, Tim Brown, wrote a breakthrough article on the topic in 2008 in the *Harvard Business Review*.[15]

Since that time, design thinking has seeped its way into every corner of Silicon Valley. The human-centered approach has helped engineers meet consumer needs and has turned fledgling startup companies into booming corporate enterprises. The process is so successful that design thinking is now applied across several industries, from packaged goods and policymaking to financial services and medicine.

Could the same level of success be found if communicators applied design thinking to their own problems?

I think yes, and it starts by deeply understanding one another.

The Power of Getting Closer

I was sixteen when I felt the power of story for the first time. It was coming on Christmas, and I was working in my first internship at a public relations firm in the suburbs of northern New Jersey. That winter, I had been tasked with telling the story of another sixteen-year-old girl living with a severe case of juvenile arthritis. She and I had much in common, but our life experiences couldn't have been more different. The condition limited her ability to walk, but this young woman was determined to run a local road race to support the Arthritis Foundation. She was determined to change the narrative that she believed others had set for her.

I met with the young woman and her family and interviewed her about her lived experiences. I saw firsthand how she had learned to not just live with her condition but to thrive in her own body—even when it wouldn't cooperate with her. As I learned her story, the perceived space between us started to close.

I pitched her story to a reporter at the *New Jersey Star-Ledger*, and one Sunday soon after, it landed on the front page. It seemed that her story resonated with far more people than just me. I remember her parents' gratitude for helping to share her story and the boost of confidence they believed it gave her to continue challenging the real and perceived limitations of her condition. She was bigger than her illness and more than her limitations—even though society didn't always see her that way. Me included.

That story challenged my attitude and response to people living with disabilities, and it continues to do so. Such is the power of story.

Disability rights activist Harriet McBryde Johnson said in the later years of her life, "Storytelling itself is an activity, not an object. Stories are the closest we can come to shared experience. Like all stories, they are most fundamentally a chance to ride around inside another head and be reminded that being who we are and where we are, and doing what we're doing, is not the only possibility."

This young woman was among my first agents of change. She was an expert by experience who showed me the power of positive storytelling to shift perceptions. Being invited to help tell her story cemented my desire to pursue a field in storytelling—the kind of storytelling that could challenge people to look and then look again at the issues.

I placed that story almost thirty years ago and still think about it every year, right around Christmas time. It's an important reminder that when we get closer to stories, we can close gaps in understanding on issues as varied as foster care, homelessness, economic mobility, mental health, and environmental justice.

To many people, narrative change is another jargon term tossed around in politics and philanthropy. To me, it's a powerful tool to shift how we interpret and understand the world around us, with the goal of making the spaces between us smaller.

BOTTOM LINE: Any number of issues can pull us apart, but people pull us together. Consider where you can get closer to people experiencing and impacted by the issues you work on, and see what it does for you as a result.

Down to the Roots

Let's go back to my friend Mauricio and a conversation I had with him and beloved impact investor Clara Miller at a small table in New Orleans back in 2014. We were together to meet a vibrant community of families who were running businesses, improving the health of their communities, preserving their heritage, and working together to strengthen their community from the inside out. They were linked together through Mauricio's work with Family Independence Initiative.

Following that trip, I wrote this reflection to Mauricio:

"A few times in my life, I've been lucky enough to feel like I was on the ground floor of something very special—something that had the potential to change the way people think, act, or engage in an effort to improve our world in some way. Not until New Orleans did I feel that I was on the ground floor of something that could change the dynamic of this country in such a powerful way."

As I noted at the beginning of this book, Mauricio's philosophy was life-focusing for me, and that trip in 2014 was a defining moment in my journey. By showcasing the value of investing in initiative, that trip directly influenced how I approach my own work and philanthropy. What I hadn't realized on that trip was just how much Mauricio's big idea has helped to define the work of others, including Clara Miller.

In a similar reflection within *Nonprofit Quarterly*,[16] Clara Miller wrote, "It wasn't that our mission—to help Americans help themselves out of poverty—needed revisiting; regrettably, that was more needed and relevant than ever. What needed some fresh thought was how we expected to achieve it and what progress we had been making thus far if any."

It's a hard but necessary question for any organization to ask: *What progress have we been making—if any?*

It's hard to know the answer to that question if we're unwilling to get down to the roots of the issue.

Both Millers—Clara and Mauricio—have been adamant about asking themselves that question, and they're working hard to ensure the answer is a good one. Clara has blazed new ground in how her foundation invests in and measures success in tackling poverty. And Mauricio continues to build momentum around his unorthodox approach to poverty alleviation, which has expanded its sights globally as hundreds of families double their savings and increase their income.

These two social innovators—each with their own unique perspective—were at the forefront of the impact investing movement. They helped define what it means to drive a mission forward. And they can be a model for how you dare to ask and how you dig into the issues, too.

Let's look at another example that proves the value of getting closer to those in our respective communities:

Alicia Bell is the co-founder of Media 2070 and director of the Racial Equity in Journalism Fund at Borealis Philanthropy. She's spent most of her career thinking about how communities engage and interact with local newsrooms, including nonprofit newsrooms. As she shared with me on our 2021 *Mission Forward* podcast, "The thing I love about news and information is that it can make the space between us smaller, and it can help us understand each other more. It can help us understand the context for what's going on around us."[17]

That's an essential insight. But what she said next still sticks with me.

"Many consumers of news I've spoken with have no relationship with their local newsrooms. But what if newsrooms found more ways to be in two-way relationships with their consumers rather than think about their readers' eyeballs on a page? When I'm doing newsroom trainings, I often tell the newsrooms, 'I am the person who you were trying to engage before...' It's a reminder that being in *actual relationship* with your stakeholders is where the best communications can start."

As Alicia so aptly points out, the de facto approach to connecting and engaging users is broken.

In marketing, an initial phase of the process includes developing personas—fictional characters created to represent a user type that might frequent a site, support a brand, or buy a product. Marketers often use personas together with very targeted market segmentation, where the qualitative personas are constructed to be representative of specific segments.

WHAT IS PERSONA DEVELOPMENT?

Persona development is the process of creating a representation of different types of people who will interact with your product or service. Personas are generally fictional characters that may possibly use your business, brand, website, or product. While helpful in theory, personas can breed stereotyping and false assumptions about your actual audience.

The challenge is that these personas are fictionalized user types fraught with assumptions. We get to decide what our persona listens to, where they shop, and what they read. In the best cases, this research is grounded in significant user research, and the personas do, in fact, represent a segment of their actual user groups.

Too often, the persona development process is a breeding ground for assumptions and bias. It's also an invitation to create space between our envisioned users and our actual users. Whoever is responsible for developing the marketing plan is also often responsible for developing the personas. The biases of this one marketing person define who the organization is, how they communicate, and how they show up in the world. In the worst-case scenarios, organizations elevate these personas to the point where the personas drive decisions rather than the actual audience driving the decisions; the true audience is never engaged.

In recent years, we've worked with dozens of organizations to take a fresh look at the audiences and personas they deem their priorities. We challenge organizations to assess the words they use with their employees and to consider *what might happen* if they break out of their comfort zones in their communications messages. Across all assignments, the greatest source of influence comes down to one word—*language*. Does your language have the desired effect on the people your brand intends to serve?

If you're ready to get closer to your audience, consider these questions:

- **What set of stakeholders most need to hear what you need to say?** Who are they, exactly and specifically? Rather than imagine the perfect persona,

Get Closer

think realistically and specifically about the intended audience.

- **What do you hope they do** with the information they learn or hear from you?

- **What do you hope will stick with them?** After you've presented your insights, will representatives of this stakeholder group be able to repeat your key messages to others in their network?

Here are a few more questions to help you determine if you're close enough to your user:

- **How often do you directly listen to and learn from your community?** This could be your donors, staff, board, or students. If you are communicating to key constituents, audiences, or stakeholders, try to be in earshot of them regularly unless you want them working on assumptions.

- **How often do you design communications in partnership with community members?** Are you regularly listening for feedback on how your communication is received?

- **How often do you ask your community of stakeholders to share their own story, in their own words?** Does this happen more or less than when you are writing and sharing stories on their behalf?

67

BOTTOM LINE: No matter how much research we have or how close we can get to our audience, communicators all make assumptions based on who we believe our community is and what they need from us. But *what if* our assumptions limit our ability to move our work forward? You'll never know if you aren't in actual relationship with your community.

Chapter 9

Embrace the Unwieldy Problems

"If I had an hour to save the world,
I'd spend fifty-five minutes defining the
problem and five minutes solving it."

ATTRIBUTED TO ALBERT EINSTEIN

Think about the last big problem you needed to solve.

If you're like most, you likely laid out the facts in front of you, asked yourself a series of questions tied to the problem, and used your analytical skills to determine the best solution. This is a very common approach to problem-solving. It's sensical, with a beginning question, middle brainstorm, and end solution.

But *what if* you aren't asking yourself the right set of questions before deciding on a solution?

In recent years, Mission Partners has advised some of the world's most well-known foundations, nonprofits, associations, and universities through some of their most pressing problems. In many of these situations, we guided organizations on reimagining their core service offerings in ways that could better benefit the community.

Through these examinations, we came to find that each group's approach to solving the problem was out of sync with its mission. Rather than thinking about what their communities needed most—and then exploring how they would best fill that need—they were looking at their problems solely through the lens of what they, as organizations, needed most.

When it comes to solving big problems, if we start with what we need and then look for someone else to help us achieve it, our chances of creating meaningful progress are slim. When we start with what others need and then create a solution that works for all sides, we are more likely to be successful.

So, rather than race to the solution, spend ample time defining the problem. Asking yourself or your team *why* you are addressing this problem is far more important than the actual solution. And, to effectively define any problem, you must spend time thinking about it from perspectives other than your own.

How often have you had the perfect solution to a problem until you put it into practice and realized the solution either couldn't be implemented or addressed the wrong problem? I suspect if you went back and analyzed why any solution failed, it may have been because you hadn't adequately thought about the problem through the lens of your consumer.

Let's head back to my opening examples about Mauricio or the nonprofit executive to see this in practice. When you go into a project with a pre-baked solution, you're likely to get the same results you've already gotten. But when you're willing to disrupt those patterns and explore different ways of addressing problems, you'll almost always get better results.

At Mission Partners, we go through this type of problem-solving daily with our clients. The start is often the same with a client telling us, in some related mix of words, "The stakes are high, and we need help getting from here to there."

As we guide each organization through the problem-solving process, we lean on the skills of design thinking—particularly on open and heart-centered communications—to help us make meaningful progress. To do that, we ask a series of probing questions, including those below, that you can ask yourself as well.

- **What are we solving for?** Can you answer this one in a way that would compel your customers to act? Don't shortchange the process of understanding and articulating why your organization matters and what it's working to achieve. As much as you think someone will support your cause, join your group, or sign up for your new course because you've got a great idea, you must be prepared with proof that your idea is real and relevant. And that means wrestling with how you're measuring your impact on the issue, too.

- **What do we stand for?** Surprisingly, most people have a much easier time answering, "What are you against?" even though the answer to the first question is at the heart of your organization's purpose and values. Once the answer is identified, and consensus among the team is reached, other business decisions start to fall more naturally into place.

- **Who's our most important customer?** As the legendary marketer Peter Drucker saw it, you have primary customers, those whose life is changed because of your work, and secondary customers, those who must be satisfied for your organization to achieve results. If you want your plan to stick, take the time to deeply understand your customer base and build a plan from their point of view. And *never, never underestimate* the importance of engaging your audience in the planning process before you even think about plotting strategy.

- **Where do others see our value?** Do you know what your primary customer would say if you asked them to define your value? Strategic planning can't happen in a vacuum, regardless of how well you think you know the answers to the questions above. Talk with enough people at least one step removed from your organization to find out how they describe your organization and its effectiveness and to uncover weaknesses or threats in your model. You'll likely find that their answers contain some of the most compelling elements of your work in a way that only an outside perspective can see.

BOTTOM LINE: Strategic problem-solving, just as in strategic communications, requires a fierce commitment to focus and a collective understanding and commitment to the ultimate goal. Start at the end of the process, and figuring out where you go from here will become much easier.

Chapter 10

Building a Dig-In Mindset

"Leadership requires two things:
a vision of the world that does not yet exist
and the ability to communicate it."

SIMON SINEK

Simon Sinek is a leadership expert and author who started a movement with his now-classic *Start with Why* book and related TED talk, "How Great Leaders Inspire Action." His movement was and is centered around asking "Why?" as a tool to get to the heart of any brand and deepen customer engagement.

Starting with *why* does, in fact, work, as it allows us to get beyond the practical nature of a question to the deeper issue behind a question. But I have found in social change communications that *what we do with the information we learn matters*. It's not enough to simply ask *why* but to dig in first to the problem and then ask *why* over and over and over again.

This sense of curiosity is what we saw in Mauricio Miller. It's what we saw in Stewart Butterfield, and it's what we've seen in dozens of social change leaders who have effectively disrupted and transformed systems. This sense of curiosity is also the basis for fostering a dig-in mindset: the type of mindset that can power movements rather than moments.

Here are three tips to put you into a dig-into-the-problem type of mindset.

1. **Clear your mind.** Start with a blank sheet of paper. Think about one person who represents your ideal consumer. The kind of person for whom you or your organization exists to serve. Draw them. Then, challenge yourself to think about what matters most to them: their life priorities, their biggest challenges, their roadblocks, and their aspirations. Where are they trying to go? Why are they unable to accomplish it? Document all you can on that piece of paper.

2. **Explore your problem from a new perspective.** Reflect on your drawing, share it with your team, and compare what you uncovered against the problem you believe needs solving. How does that sheet of paper change how you think about the problem? And if you were to put that person at the center of your strategy, what else might change?

3. **Ask why; then ask it again.** To get to the heart of the problem that *really* needs solving, don't just ask yourself *why* once. As we outlined above, ask yourself *why* multiple times, and with each answer you write down, you'll get closer to the root of the problem. Once you've uncovered the root-level *why* you have a much better chance of defining *how* to solve a problem, and that's where so much of the magic happens.

Here's an example of how this process of getting to the root-level *why* played out in 2013 for the Jim Casey Youth Opportunities Initiative, which advances policies and practices to meet the needs of young people transitioning from foster care to adulthood:

- Question: *Why do we need a better path for young people aging out of foster care?*

- Answer: *Because every day, young people are aging out of care on their eighteenth birthday without the skills, support systems, or sense of self that is required for them to be successful in life.*

- Root-Level Question: *Why don't we focus on providing those skills before they age out of care?*

- Root-Level Answer: *Because most young people—in foster care or otherwise—aren't ready to be self-sufficient adults by their eighteenth birthday. They need to get beyond their eighteenth birthday to be fully equipped with the skills required for success.*

This last answer raised a deeper question for us all. Were we solving for re-imagining the foster care system as it was, or re-imagining how it *should* work—with far more supports beyond a young person's eighteenth birthday than previously expected?

That root-level question and the corresponding answer became the basis of our work with the Jim Casey Youth Opportunities Initiative. It also spurred our work in building a national campaign called Success Beyond 18, now heralded in child welfare circles as a key driver in the passage of Public

Law 113-183—The Preventing Sex Trafficking and Strengthening Families Act.

By asking why until we reached the root cause of the problem, we were able to build a campaign with much deeper staying power. But we had to be willing to ask why and dig into the unwieldy problem.

BOTTOM LINE: We're all designers, even if it's not in our job title. We control how our programs, initiatives, and organizations are presented. Acknowledge the great power and responsibility in that. We influence how stories are told, who tells them, who's included... and who's overlooked.

Chapter 11

Autopilot Is for Cars, Not Communicators

"Every single one of us, celebrity or not,
has a responsibility to get involved in trying
to make a difference in the world...
it's up to us to find solutions today so that
we don't keep passing our problems on."

SHAKIRA

Given my line of work as a social impact communicator working with nonprofit organizations, I receive many fundraising appeals from nonprofit organizations. In other words, I'm on the receiving end of many asks: fundraising appeals, annual reports, and marketing materials—some very well-produced and others less so.

A few years ago, I found an interesting formula that kept playing out in these nonprofit appeals:

- They started with a story

- They described what the individual or family needed

- They show how the organization saved the day

- And then they ask for money

Perhaps that's the *obvious* way of asking for money: tell me a story, show me why it matters, tell me what my impact will be, and then lay your question on me. But something hasn't sat well with me about this formula for a while.

It clicked recently when I received a solicitation from one well-intended social service nonprofit organization. The words attempted to communicate one thing, but how the words were presented communicated another.

- **What I saw when I opened the envelope:** An image of an older Black man in his seventies, who appeared unbathed and disheveled. His hair was matted down from a baseball hat he held in his hand, and his button-down shirt had a tear in the side pocket. The picture was grainy, and the poor quality presented the man in an even harsher light.

- **What I read:** The man was down on his luck until he got connected with this nonprofit. The nonprofit provided food, shelter, and supportive services to help his recovery process. Now, he was back on his own, reunited with his children, and holding a consistent job.

- **What I felt:** Deep concern and empathy for the man and concern about the nonprofit. This mailing didn't elicit trust or a willingness to give. It raised concern over how this particular nonprofit aimed to profit from one man's story. I couldn't tell if he approved of the story, if he had been compensated for telling his story, or if he even knew his story was being used in this way. A highly effective and evocative model was lost on me through the communication presentation.

I suspect the intention was good and well-placed. But in an effort to put a human face on the campaign, the team behind the marketing material dehumanized the man at the center of their story.

Using success stories to help further our mission has been a tried-and-true nonprofit fundraising strategy for decades. In many cases, it's the normal and expected way of doing business. But, as I shared in the opening story of this book and as Ed Yong said in the context of COVID-19, "normal led us to this."

For people working to create change in communities, communication often happens on autopilot—from appeals that center on the stories of beneficiaries to fancy galas that require success stories to be featured on center stage. All these stories are told in ways that will elicit big money from donors.

In practice, these actions are successful. They raise the money needed to advance the mission. But it leaves me to wonder: what is the point? Is it the nonprofit's job to maintain these services uninterrupted to care for those in the community? Or is their job to take on—even if just scratching the surface—the root causes that require these services to be needed in the first place?

Stewart Butterfield and his team at Slack didn't set out to advance the status quo. They saw an opportunity to disrupt it. And they used communications as their tool to advance that social change. I believe you can, too.

Keep reading into our third practice for tools that break storytelling autopilot.

> **BOTTOM LINE:** The language we build inside the walls of our organizations is often designed with specific audiences in mind. That can lead to dangerous consequences if we don't stop to consider how our language sits with those outside of our respective comfort zones. Who understands our message, and who feels left out? Even worse, who is receiving an unintended negative message?

Widen Your Lens

"If you change the way you look at things,
the things you look at change."

DR. WAYNE DYER

One of the important disruptions I've adopted in my work is reevaluating how stories are framed and from what perspective they're told. The people and stories featured in this book section have influenced *how* I tell stories and how I teach and train others to do the same.

This third practice requires that we consider the power of our words and actions to move people, organizations, and issues forward. It requires that we understand the intended and unintended impact of our communications. We have the power, which we must acknowledge, to address, disrupt, and dismantle false or toxic narratives that limit social progress from taking hold.

These lessons are not about swapping one word for another but shifting the frame altogether for long-term change. These lessons are about being present, being intentional, and being human-centered. As you'll see in the coming pages, the communications that happen on autopilot are often the communications that do the most harm.

To communicate effectively, we need to acknowledge that the people we're speaking with—the humans at the receiving end of our messages—are just as important as the words we use. But we also realize that the human element of communicating can be the most difficult element to master.

As you start the third practice, consider these guiding questions and revisit your answers after completing the book.

THINK ABOUT THIS. Think of a time that your communications reinforced biases. Rewrite that scenario with what you might say or do differently today.

WRITE THIS DOWN. How open are you to embracing change in your communications planning and listening process?

Chapter 12

Stories for Social Change

"The single story creates stereotypes, and the problem with stereotypes is not that they aren't true, but they are incomplete. They make one story become the only story."

CHIMAMANDA NGOZI ADICHIE

A few years ago, I worked with a college readiness program to produce a video for their annual gala. To help inform the content, I interviewed a dozen recent college graduates about their experiences getting to and through college. I heard many powerful stories that day, but the passion and presence of one young woman stood out. She shared how low self-esteem and a lack of a consistent support system had instilled in her a sense of doubt and limited her from pursuing her love of art. Then she shared the moment everything changed. She found an art teacher who believed in her talents and supported her dream to pursue a college degree in design. As she sat across from me, she was a newly minted college graduate with a full-time job in a field she loved.

To her, that *was* the fairy-tale ending she could have never dreamed of as a child.

It was, by all accounts, a success story. She had done everything that the organization I was working with aimed to support—ensuring that students with limited access to financial resources had pathways to higher education to achieve their higher purpose. She would make for a great start to the gala's activities.

I scheduled a call to review my findings and recommendations with our client, though I wasn't prepared for their reaction.

"Oh, that will never work. She's in an arts field. We should really be highlighting young men and women in the STEM fields, as those jobs are so much more lucrative and will elicit more donations from our tech sector guests."

The person speaking found something lacking—even negative—about pursuing an arts job over a tech job. Their preference to lead with stories that could elicit the most donations got in the way of fully supporting and celebrating this young woman for all she had overcome. We did manage to get her story in the show's lineup, but it didn't take the lead spot as I wished.

I frequently think about that experience and wonder just how often our biases—our own misplaced happy-ending stories—get in the way of seeing the full potential of the people around us.

I'm reminded of my conversation with Pulitzer Prize-winning science journalist Ed Yong, who, as I mentioned in an earlier chapter, shared with me the moment he first observed gender bias in his writing and how we went about addressing it. As Ed and I discussed, bias can get in the way of us observing the full picture. But we can choose to acknowledge it and work to address it.

To help us get to the big picture, let's zoom out and touch on a few basics of storytelling.

- **What we already know:** A story tells us about an event or series of events, either real or fictional. Stories are told to interest, entertain, and teach us. Stories help us connect with others, communicate ideas, and imagine life's possibilities. Even the most basic stories have a beginning, middle, and end.

- **What we tend to forget:** Stories hold great power in shaping how we view and understand the world and, more specifically, the people around us.

It is all too common for a nonprofit to start its newsletter with a story of someone at risk, vulnerable, or needing support. Somehow, we've been taught these are the stories we need to tell to engage our donors and supporters.

But *what if* we changed that frame? I think we can, and it starts by understanding our audience and the power of our word.

To see this practice in action, let's look at some work we did a few years back with a 150-year-old New York City-based organization called The New York Foundling. When they reached out to us, they had recently gone through a visual rebrand, but the messages were still falling flat. They were leaning on old messages that no longer reflected how their approach to the work, and the people they supported, had evolved. They realized the power of updating their words to increase their effectiveness.

So, we got smart on New York Foundling's stakeholders and audiences. We explored who they were and what mattered to them—not as personas but as actual stakeholders. With their audiences in mind, we had a focal point by which to reimagine their core messages.

Here's where they started:

> Established by the Sisters of Charity as a home for abandoned babies in 1869, The Foundling has grown into one of New York City's leading child welfare organizations. Through evidence-based and evidence-informed programming across a wide range of service areas, we pursue our central mission: to empower children and families struggling with poverty and lack of social opportunity to live healthy, independent, and fulfilling lives.

Using brand science and community-informed research, we wanted to challenge their language to be more strengths-based and accurate. We wanted to honor their past while opening the door to their future. This wasn't a story about abandoned babies or children who needed empowerment. It was a story of children and families who mattered and systems that were letting them down. We needed to tell the whole story rather than a single story.

Here's where we landed:

> The New York Foundling is built on a 150-year-old promise to our neighbors that all children, adults, and families can have the opportunity to reach their full potential. As one of New York's longest-serving nonprofit organizations, we are both established and innovative, people-centered, and data-driven. With an effective and interrelated set of services, The New York Foundling works in partnership with its neighbors on their own paths to stability, strength, and independence.

> - We help children and families navigate through and beyond foster care.
>
> - We help families struggling with conflict and poverty to grow stronger.
>
> - We help individuals with differing abilities to live their best lives.
>
> - Our health and mental health services— core to building lifelong resilience—remove obstacles to wellbeing.

Words make a difference. By broadening the story, we also broadened the organization's value to staff and supporters. The stories that followed these words became more inclusive, more open, more honest, and more effective. Once The

New York Foundling realized they didn't need to stick to the old frame, they started to see what was possible for their future and how they advanced their work through communications. Communications became a central part of their strategy rather than an add-on. And that's when we knew they had learned storytelling as a tool for social change.

The Equity Impact Analysis Tool[18]

> Consider what effect your words and stories have on your community. Consider where you are telling a partial story versus the whole story. To help guide you through this, use our equity impact analysis tool to see how well your current communications are faring.

When developing communication tactics, policies, and/or practices, consider the following questions throughout the process.

What is the impact?

How will this communication potentially affect each group? Consider the impact you hope to have and the unintended impact your work could have on your audience.

What's the data?

Does it worsen or ignore existing disparities? Seek out the data and ask for feedback.

Can you listen closer?

What strategies are being used, and how will you challenge yourself to radically listen to those affected and incorporate feedback as you move forward? Check for bias and assumptions.

Can you close the gaps?

Does it work to close the gaps in racial disparities in culturally appropriate, inclusive ways? If not, how should it be revised? If so, how can it be documented to offer a model for others?

Is everyone at the table?

Are all the community members who are influenced—particularly those who are often least heard—represented at the decision-making table? Do people feel engaged and valued enough to speak? Are you considering other underrepresented communities as well?

BOTTOM LINE: As you think about the stories you tell, the ones you'll pass down, and the ones you share in your work, ask yourself if you're creating the conditions to tell the whole story—not just the story you think people want to hear. Then ask, over and over again, who is missing from this narrative?

Chapter 13

Retool the Frame

"The injustices are real.
Don't ignore any of them.
But don't define anyone by them either.
Injustice is not what defines anyone."

TRABIAN SHORTERS

In the first chapter of this book, I shared how my journey to understand the power of communications came to a head in 2016 when I realized that my storytelling style had become part of the problem and was limiting positive social change from taking hold. With the best of intentions, I had been perpetuating harmful, false, and toxic narratives rather than disrupting, challenging, or reimagining those narratives. Not all our work was ruinous, but I realized it could be better. It needed to be better. Because I knew better.

One of the people who planted an early seed of this for me was Jacques, a high schooler from West Philadelphia who I first met in 2008. Jacques was part of a high school team competing against global behemoths for the $10M Progressive Insurance Automotive XPRIZE. The global prize competition was hosted by the XPRIZE Foundation—my client at the time—who uses the power of prize competitions to un-stick some of the world's most intractable problems. And between 2007 and 2010, that problem was America's addiction to oil. The XPRIZE Foundation dangled $10M to engineers, automakers, garage inventors, and even a few high schoolers who set out together to find a better solution for powering automobiles.

Jacques and his high school teammates were the underdogs. But that's also why their story caught the attention of the national and international press. After securing them a print magazine feature, I received a call from a top national broadcast outlet that wished to do a long-form interview with the team. This was a dream come true for the students and a great win for the XPRIZE. I traveled to Philadelphia to oversee the taping. For an entire day, the students showed off their technology and answered questions, soaking up the excitement of this moment. And then, a few hours into the taping, the group sat down for a more serious conversation. The reporter, who started with a lighthearted conversation, quickly shifted into a line of questioning we hadn't expected. She wanted to know what life was like for these students on the tough streets of inner-city Philadelphia. She wanted to know how many of them saw guns, drugs, and fights in school and how those experiences shaped their desire to run after this multimillion-dollar prize. But before she could fully shape the narrative she was focused on building, Jacques stepped in.

"That's not it at all," he said. "There might be days that are tough here, but that's no different from any city high school." He went on to remind the reporter that the story she was here to cover was about a group of brilliant and creative high school kids breaking barriers that no other kids on the planet had been able to do.

And with that, he had changed the frame. He had found the words that she needed to change the trajectory of that story.

A few years after meeting Jacques, I came to understand more clearly what he had done from Trabian Shorters, CEO of the BMe Community and one of the world's leading social entrepreneurs and the catalyst of a national movement to define Black people by their aspirations and contributions, rather than by the deficits of their communities.

As Trabian notes, "Human beings are hardwired to create and act upon narratives. We crave the moral direction stories provide. And whether we know it or not, we constantly default to these narratives, which often place White men at the front of history."

What Jacques had done wasn't just brave. It was essential.

And with a more formal understanding, I started to see the possibilities of a new approach to storytelling.

That more formal understanding came to me through Trabian Shorter's Asset-Framing model, which defines people by their assets and aspirations before noting the challenges and deficits.

Case in point:

- **The deficit frame:** an at-risk teen with little to no chance of making it to college

- **The asset frame:** an aspiring college student navigating the limited options available in their community

The difference between starting a story by talking about an at-risk teen versus starting a story by talking about an aspiring college student does more for behavior change than you might even imagine. Because of culture, media, and society, our brains have learned to associate "student" with *potential* and "at-risk" with *problem*. The words matter, and by starting with more asset-based framing, we can help the reader see the full story and connect with the full person.

As Shorters explained during a conversation with Krista Tippett on the *On Being* podcast, "The primary mind, which does ninety-five percent of our mental work, is intuitive. How it is primed determines how it perceives situations, people, and systems because priming determines which narratives and data we will credit and which ones we'll discredit or ignore."[19]

Going a step further, asset-based framing aims to give our primary mind a fuller set of information and associations to draw upon when making decisions. It is an essential cognitive skill for priming associations of genuine "worth" rather than priming fear as our sole motivator for equitable action.

A good practice in asset-framing is to state what you want—your prime hope—twice as often as you state what you don't want—your prime fear. This is because our minds hold on to fear stimuli longer and more easily, so a fifty-fifty split does not sufficiently outweigh fear prompting.

Heading back to those early days of C.Fox Communications, I remember relying on words like "voiceless," "at-risk," and "vulnerable" too often. The fact that I was relying on them at all, quite frankly, was a failure. But we were also not alone. In the mid-2000s, deficit-based frames had become pervasive in our field. We were on autopilot, using communications tactics and techniques that were industry standard but far from socially beneficial.

Drawing forward from Trabian Shorters' work, I also started to explore and research the power of frames through asset-based and deficit-based framing, which again I credit to my earliest days of working with Mauricio Miller.

In asset-based framing, we help the brains of our readers and viewers gain the broadest understanding of the main characters through a lens of aspirations rather than deficits. Yet often, in nonprofit and social sector storytelling, the default is deficit-framing. Over time, deficit-framing can create cynicism and eat away at hope.

As Trabian Shorters helped me understand, defining people by their challenges is stigmatizing. When using or being exposed to deficit-framing, our brains begin to match negative qualities to certain people or groups, which has deeply harmful cognitive and social consequences.

Table. Examining the difference between asset-based and deficit-based frames.

ASSET-BASED	DEFICIT-BASED
• Strengths driven	• Needs driven
• Opportunity focused	• Problems focused
• Internally focused	• Externally focused
• What is present that we can build on?	• What is missing that we must find?
• May lead to new, unexpected responses to community wishes	• May lead to a downward spiral of burnout, depression, or dysfunction

Asset-framing acknowledges that people and experiences are complex.

Drawing from the basic frames outlined above, we can then pull out further to understand how stories come together, and to do that, let's head back to the work we did with the Jim Casey Youth Opportunities Initiative and their Success Beyond 18 campaign.

Start with the common experience, not the stereotype.

Think with me about the moment that you turned eighteen. Now think about what it would have been like to be handed a garbage bag with your basic belongings and left on your own. No job, no home, no car. That's the experience that nearly every young person in foster care experiences on their eighteenth birthday. But it doesn't have to be that way.

To a young person in foster care, turning eighteen can be scary. In one day, they must shift from having little say in their life to being on their own. Not surprisingly, they face many challenges.

Consider the possible outcome, not the perceived challenge.

New research shows interventions during adolescence can make a difference. Contrary to popular belief, adolescent brain development provides another window of opportunity similar to early childhood brain development. We know that it is possible to achieve better outcomes for young people. Young people themselves are advocating for change, but they need your help. We need the political will and leadership required to make the necessary improvements.

The research tells us what challenges they will almost certainly face in the next few years if we continue doing business as usual. We also know they are resilient and can succeed with the right support.

> "Let me tell you about a successful young person I know…"

What we learned from Trabian Shorters' work and applied during our Success Beyond 18 campaign was that the most compelling stories for social change break the stereotypes of children living in foster care. They challenge the stereotypes of a child welfare system. And they reframe the story in a way that centers the aspirations versus the deficits of young people. Inherently Jacques knew this too.

Consider the following prompts to see how you show up as a storyteller for social change.

Action Steps for Eliminating Bias and Advancing Equity in Communications

COMPENSATION

If you have featured an individual or family in any of your publications in the past year, how often have you compensated them for sharing their story, given the way you use their story to drive resources to your organization's bottom line? And the bigger question is: what is your organization's policy for compensating community storytellers?

REVIEW

Are the people highlighted in your fundraising appeals allowed to review and edit their stories? How many people have you asked to fact-check their success stories? How might the story look different if you had? And again, the bigger question is: what is your organization's policy for reviewing materials before they are published? Who gets to hold that red editing pen, and who doesn't?

PERSPECTIVE

Rather than feeling tied to the frame set out above, what do you think might happen if you flipped the narrative to a different perspective? What voice other than the carefully crafted executive director or beneficiary could you consider that compellingly delivers your message?

VOICE

When was the last time you connected with your community? Not on your terms, but on theirs. We all make assumptions based on who we believe our community is and what they need. To reduce those assumptions, evaluate how often you authentically connect with your community, asking them to share their own narrative in their own way. How often are you asking your community if they feel adequately and factually represented in your marketing materials?

These are tough questions and not standard for most nonprofit organizations. But, if you believe that equity and inclusion are important to your organizational culture, the actions you take on the above questions are ways to prove your commitment.

> **BOTTOM LINE:** We all have something to say, and we all want to be heard. But for many of us, *how* we say what needs to be said will determine our audience's ability to hear us.

Chapter 14

Start at the Top

"Words and ideas
can change the world."

ROBIN WILLIAMS

When it comes to telling stories or describing initiatives designed for long-term social change, it's not just about the words we use but how we use them.

I've often used a very basic metaphor to help explain this principle. First, think of a basic triangle upside down, so the point of the triangle is on the bottom. This is the way most of us speak.

We are permitted an opportunity to talk about something we love or are passionate about, and so we talk. And eventually, we make our point.

If we are lucky, our audience—be it a donor, a colleague, a policymaker, or a friend—is still listening when we make that point. It feels effective, like we've amplified our message. But the truth is, most of the message is lost on the audience. That's because talking *at* someone before we eventually get to our point isn't how our brains process information. In this framework, as the user, we are lost, trying to decipher what someone is saying to us or where they are going.

That's not the case when you flip the triangle upside down. When you start with your point—the most essential and obvious point you need to make and the point you need your audience to hear—and then build from that initial point into a supporting story, facts, or context, then the reader or listener can follow along. They better understand what you're communicating and why.

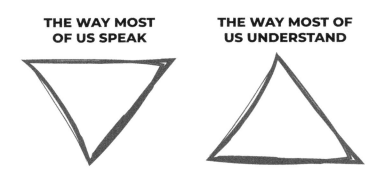

THE WAY MOST OF US SPEAK

THE WAY MOST OF US UNDERSTAND

Starting at the top—expressing the most important point first—and working your way into the conversation can help your audience process difficult or complicated information. It gives your listeners context to help them understand the bigger issues. That word, context, is essential. And as you'll see coming into this portion of the book, the more specific and focused your stories, the better the tool they'll be for you.

To explore this more closely, let's head back in time for a moment to 2013. My team and I had just started consulting with a Boston-based nonprofit called Children's HealthWatch.

Founded in 1998 by Drs. Deborah A. Frank, Diana B. Cutts, Patrick Casey, Maureen M. Black, and Carol Berkowitz, and led by a team of pediatric clinicians and researchers, the organization focuses specifically on the impacts of economic and social factors on very young children. Their work shines an essential spotlight on the challenges this population faces during the most crucial years of their cognitive and physical development. Their work over these past twenty-five years has been extraordinary.

However, when we first met them, their message was muddled. As pediatric providers, they were as close as they could get to the problem. That wasn't the issue. In fact, they knew their user better than anyone else. But their messages got lost when the team tried to take their recommendations to Capitol Hill to advocate for policy change.

When they hired us, here's exactly how they described their communications problem: "We can't seem to translate our messages in a way that inspires action. We need to convey to policymakers that we have a disaster in America affecting our youngest children, but it's fixable with the right resources and focus. We can get meetings with people in positions of power, but when we tell our story, their eyes glaze over!"

I can't tell you how many times I've heard that last part—about an audience's eyes *glazing over*. And I bet you can relate. Just think back to a time when you were overly confident heading into a presentation and then reflected after it was over and said to yourself or your colleagues, "What just happened?"

Over the course of a few engagements, we helped Children's HealthWatch reframe its story so that feeling wouldn't happen again, and we started at the top of the triangle by asking *what if*?

- *What if* we committed to ending childhood hunger by building up—not tearing down—public infrastructures that offer our nation's children the best chance at successful adulthood?

- Using the most current data on food insecurity and poverty, we can change the current policy conversation about childhood hunger by showing the social and financial benefits tied to strengthening—not just maintaining—existing federal nutrition programs.

By demonstrating how building upon existing federal nutrition programs today benefits us all tomorrow, Children's HealthWatch no longer delivered their story in a way that beat up their audiences. Instead, they presented an open door to a more inclusive, productive dialogue about ending childhood hunger in America.

Then, we took that *what if* frame and built a story that mattered to the audience around it:

> Think about where you grew up—your neighborhood, your proximity to good schools, doctors' offices, healthy food, access to transportation options, and community programs. Think about how access to those things—or the lack of access—shaped who you are. For many of us, the word home likely conjures up memories and emotions that make us feel good, even if we didn't have that

experience ourselves. But home is so much more. Consistent, stable, and affordable homes in connected communities are a prescription for good health. Families are more likely to be healthy, and their children are more likely to thrive when resources exist beyond the mortgage or rent payment to invest in health, education, and wellbeing.

However, more than one-third of U.S. households still find themselves choosing every month between paying the rent and paying for the health-related costs of their children.

If funding and policy changes refocused the resources currently spent on downstream health effects—related to lack of access to affordable homes and poor-quality housing— we could significantly decrease the number of Americans experiencing serious, costly health issues. Investing in consistent, stable housing for children now is a prescription for good health in the future.

This narrative shift—seeing the problem as part of the solution—allowed the pediatric researchers at Children's HealthWatch to tap into a different part of the story. The *heart* of the story. It allowed them to connect with the powerful decision-makers, in this case, elected government members on multiple levels, opening doors to new and different types of funding. In the end, the narrative wasn't about what was broken in the system. It was about what could be done to collectively improve the system.

As you're building the frame of your story, here are some prompts that may help:

- **Start with the big picture.** What is your most important point, and will it matter to your audience?

- **Tell your audience why this matters now.** Address the urgency of this issue and how it resonates with the audience.

- **Show where and how you fit into the story.** Use stories and anecdotes.

- **Prove it.** Facts and stories bring an interview to life and make the listener care.

- **Know where to land.** What is the most important takeaway? Reinforce a point from the start of the conversation.

BOTTOM LINE: By asking *what if* and transforming the expected "broken" frame into a possibilities mindset, we can open the doors to conversations that were previously closed.

Follow Through

"Storytelling itself is an activity, not an object. Stories are the closest we can come to shared experience...

They are most fundamentally a chance to ride around inside another head and be reminded that being who we are and where we are, and doing what we're doing, is not the only possibility."

HARRIET MCBRYDE JOHNSON

Throughout this book, I've said many times that as communicators, our designs—otherwise known as our decisions—directly affect others.

The problem, however, is that we often design with the same people at our tables and with the same biases we carry through life. We often design for what we know, see, and understand as the problem without comprehending or addressing the full scope of the problem. And as a result, many people—historically, those without traditional positions of power or influence—are left out of the design and decision-making process. The results are strategies that fall short and marketing materials that cause more harm than good.

What would happen if we could listen, learn, and act more intentionally across whatever divides us? If we changed how we look at things, might we be able to recognize biases and inequities more easily and therefore have the power to disrupt them?

In this fourth principle, we'll focus on developing the practices and tools designed to guide your journey as a communicator for change, including how you personally show up as a communicator.

Whether you're the spokesperson today or responsible for managing the spokesperson, we all play a role in moving our respective missions forward. Being well-equipped in the moment to address hard questions sets a foundation of success for your organization and you.

As you head into the final principle, consider these prompts:

THINK ABOUT THIS. If you're looking to change systems, advance social justice, or leave the world better than you found it, think about what you might change in your own communication style to help make it happen. You don't need to have all the answers, but you do need to show you care. In the end, that will be remembered most.

WRITE THIS DOWN. Who are the people that practice courageous communications in your life? What might you draw from their best practices into your own work and communications style?

Chapter 15

Real, Relatable, Repeatable

> "When you experience mercy, you learn
> things that are hard to learn otherwise.
> You see things you can't otherwise see;
> you hear things you can't otherwise hear.
> You begin to recognize the humanity
> that resides in each of us."
>
> BRYAN STEVENSON

Think about the last request you made of someone that went unanswered. Maybe it was to a colleague, a potential funder, or a journalist.

Why do you think they didn't respond?

Maybe the request came in at a bad time. Maybe it was communicated on the wrong platform, buried in an inbox, or left on a voicemail that's rarely checked. Or maybe the message itself was just plain off. Not relevant. Not interesting. Not understood.

According to a survey of nonprofit communicators, more than seven out of ten nonprofits describe their messaging as feeling "off target." Those same communicators are at a loss for how to adjust their messages for increased "stickiness."

The good news is that those who receive regular and positive responses to their requests all have three little things in common with their messaging: they are real, they're relatable, and they're repeatable. Great communicators can articulate their requests in such a way that others embrace them freely and feel compelled to provide support.

So, where do most communicators go wrong? They bury their headlines. They bury their why—the reason that this message matters and the reason it matters now. Instead of articulating that core message right up front, it gets buried in paragraph after paragraph of conversation and copy.

As referenced in the prior chapter, simply inverting the conversation and leading with the most imperative point, matters. Otherwise, by the time the ask is made, the audience is almost always long gone. Stories matter, but how the stories are told matters even more.

As you think about your approach to storytelling, remember this:

- We are humans first, so speak in language that all humans, and not just those in your sector, will understand.

- Then, help us see how your story connects to the bigger world around us. Consider the intersections of your issue with other critical issues of our time.

- Finally, consider how you might deliver your message in a style that will stick with someone, even in a form that someone will repeat to another.

Over the last several years of watching how people communicate, I've learned that three kinds of messages, as detailed above, truly spur action. Simply put, we must make our stories real, relatable, and repeatable. And when used together, the power of this message trifecta truly comes to life.

Make it   **Make it**   **Make it**
Real   **Relatable**   **Repeatable**

MAKE IT REAL

We are humans first. Stories are a way to make your content simple, interesting, and emotional. Given that our minds are wired to understand information through stories, people are more likely to pay attention to the things that appeal to them rather than things that do not. And they're more likely to remember and recall what they do pay attention to rather than what they do not. So, put the technical jargon aside, and speak to your audience as you would speak to a friend. Some individuals believe that the more complex their message, the more impressive. But just the opposite is true. The simpler you can make your messages, the more compelling they will be.

MAKE IT RELATABLE

After twenty years of pitching stories to the media, I've gotten pretty used to hearing, "Tell me why *this* story matters." What's different about this story, and why should your audience care? Sharing a message that touches on life experience or hits someone in their heart is about separating the *what* of the message from the background noise. Separating out the *what* leads to the *why*—your core message and the big picture. Relatability occurs when a story is conveyed simply, logically, and in a way that resonates with people's lived experiences.

Relatable messages are those that people hold on to; they're the kind of messages that tap into people's heads and hearts simultaneously. Relatability is also a vital door opener to any conversation. Be sure to show that you're in sync with what's happening in your audience's world and that you understand where you fit into their agenda. Do this well, and you'll find your audience turning into your best advocates and allies.

MAKE IT REPEATABLE.

Stickiness is a quality of memorability; it attracts and holds attention. People find it easier to remember things that make a lasting impression on them—things that "stick" in their minds, such as the right word and the right phrase, especially when spelled out by the right character in the right context. So, feed your audience a good story that proves why they should care. Stories help people who are less familiar with your work understand its importance, but they also provide a ready-made vehicle to get others talking. Tell a story that helps bring the importance of your message to life, and it is much more likely to be remembered and repeated.

So, to get your next important message to stick, ask yourself the following before you hit send:

- **Is it Real?** Are my words simple and understandable?

- **Is it Relatable?** Have I clarified why I'm asking now and what kind of impact potential support could make?

- **Is it Repeatable?** Have I done a good enough job proving myself? Have I included a story or anecdote that reinforces my point compellingly?

> **BOTTOM LINE:** Making our stories real, relatable, and repeatable is a formula for effective and lasting change. And when used together, the power of this message trifecta truly comes to life.

Chapter 16

Authenticity, Specificity, and Agency

> "What we know matters but who we are matters more."
>
> BRENÉ BROWN

Over the years, I've learned that being a communicator for change requires being willing to ask hard questions, being willing to dig into unwieldy problems, and being willing to look at situations from new perspectives. All those skills help to inform strategies and stories that can lead to social change.

Just as the story matters, so does the storyteller. In this next section, let's look at the specific keys to effective storytelling to ensure that a message is heard, remembered, and passed along.

First, let me tell you a story.

In March 2022, director Jane Campion accepted a Critics Choice award onstage for her work on the film *The Power of the Dog*. Campion could have used her precious seconds onstage to celebrate the nominees or inspire future female directors. Instead, she used the moment to undermine the accomplishments of tennis legends Venus and Serena Williams, whose lives were the basis for the movie *King Richard*, another nominated film.

"*Serena and Venus, you are such marvels. However, you don't play against the guys like I have to.*"

Her comment was harmful and oblivious. From the looks of the video and the corresponding wave of media coverage,[20] she had no idea what she had just done.

But what we do—and say—with our precious moments matters. I suspect you, too, have gotten caught up in the moment and unintentionally said something you soon regretted.

It happens all the time. People in high-profile moments and small group meetings aim to make the most of a moment. But our words and actions don't always land the way we intend.

What to do when it happens to you? Start by understanding the difference between intent and impact:

- **Intent:** is what you have in mind when you decide to act; it becomes your intention. Your intent reflects what type of impact you want to create with your actions.

- **Impact:** is the result of intentional actions. Results may not necessarily align with your intentions. Impact reflects the reality of your actions.

If your good intentions have led to unintended consequences, take time to recognize the disconnect. You meant one thing, but your words caused something else. Rather than jump to the defensive, pause, and acknowledge your words' effect.

Acknowledging impact versus intent starts with the self-awareness to recognize when an adverse effect has occurred. It is followed by showing the strength of character to admit your fault. It requires authenticity, specificity, and agency—three skills that don't always come easily.

Let's take a closer look at authenticity, specificity, and agency.

AUTHENTICITY

Stories that truly persuade are about "One person, one problem, one point." We often refer to populations in the aggregate—as a big group rather than an individual who wants to receive a personalized message. We will only get our audience to empathize with us through one character at a time.

For example, let's head back to my work with the Jim Casey Youth Opportunities Initiative. A youth-led effort to reimagine the foster care system required youth leaders. Executives trying to tell the story of how the system was broken, particularly those who had never experienced the foster care system, might be somewhat compelling. But a story told by young people drawing on their experience offers a first-hand account of the system's failures from the people who have lived it most closely.

Keep in mind not every leader has the appetite to move out of the spokesperson role in favor of letting someone else, particularly a young person, speak. You may be among them. But I can tell you from experience that authentic stories are hard to match, and authenticity can, in fact, live in more places than the executive office.

SPECIFICITY

Storytelling is about more than the numbers. Numbers and aggregate measures don't mean anything in storytelling. If we recall Lisa Cron's book, she said, "If you can't see it, you can't feel it. If you can't feel it, you won't be inspired to take action." Be specific in your stories; don't expect data to do all the heavy lifting for you.

For example, scientists know about eight million metric tons of plastic are dumped into the world's oceans annually, creating a huge environmental problem and a life-threatening hazard to marine life. Yet, it wasn't until people saw the story of a sea turtle with a single straw painfully wedged up its nose that a worldwide movement to ban plastic straws finally took hold. It took that one story to capture people's hearts.

When telling stories to inspire people to *do* something—give money, write their representative, visit a website for more information, et cetera—real-life, emotional examples must support the numbers. It's the only way you make your audience stop, listen, and care.

AGENCY

Telling and owning our own stories is essential. If we focus on telling someone else's story, we risk losing trust, credibility, and any shot of real or lasting change. We must own our own stories.

For example, Ronald Johnson is a lifetime advocate for the HIV community. His career spans more than three decades of leadership in policy and advocacy to improve our response to the HIV epidemic, to keep people living with HIV healthy, and to prevent new infections. He was among the first people openly living with HIV to serve in public office. In 1992, when he was forty-four, Ronald was named by Mayor David Dinkins to serve as New York City's first coordinator for AIDS policy, where he helped strengthen HIV care and treatment across the city. Ronald understood early that to be an effective advocate and activist, he needed to start with his own story of being a young Black gay man who came of age just before the 1969 Stonewall riots. He leaned on his personal history to challenge existing narratives about AIDS and open the door for deeper discussions about the issue, as he did with a CNN editorial I helped him place in 2012.[21] In his words, "The first and foremost reason I remain in HIV work is because I am a person living with HIV," he says. "But I also remain involved because HIV/AIDS continues to be a major health crisis here in the U.S. and around the world."

By starting with his story, Ronald has been able to help his audiences—elected officials and policymakers among them—understand the hard statistics more personally: only 19 percent of Americans living with HIV receive the sustained care they need; 1.2 million Americans live with HIV. His own experiences drove him to enter this work, and his personal stories have helped shape some of the current policies to support people living with HIV and AIDS.

When you're thinking about using storytelling as a device, consider these prompts:

- **Who is the intended audience?** Be clear.

- **How do you want them to feel?** Choose action-oriented emotions.

- **What do you want them to do?** Be specific.

- **What is your connection to the issue?** Be authentic.

- **Who is the character at the center of the story?** Increase involvement by incorporating your own story and experience.

BOTTOM LINE: Acknowledging intent over impact takes practice, but the good news is even in moments of poor judgment, we can turn something bad into something good again.

Chapter 17

Challenge Your Assumptions

> "Your assumptions are your
> windows on the world.
> Scrub them off every once in a while,
> or the light won't come in."
>
> ALAN ALDA

Picking up on our prior chapter, what you say and how you say it are equally important. However, the message is only one factor in success. Sounding like a robot delivering the corporate line won't do much for building trust or credibility. Turns out, the actual words matter a lot less than you might think. No one's ever said that the key to effective communications is to sound more robotic or to memorize the corporate line.

Your words won't matter if nothing is behind them.

Delivering a message that matters—a message that can move masses forward—always works best when delivered from the heart. And that matters today more than ever.

Assumption Breakers and Accountability Partners

A few years ago, I began hosting Design Thinking Days at Mission Partners for our community. Every few months, we convened a small group of curious people who each agreed to look closely at their current communications practices to see where the greatest gaps in their communications existed. We explored the types of gaps preventing their audiences from hearing, believing, and acting on those communications.

We'd always start the same way, by looking at assumptions.

Assumptions are baked into so much of what we do and so many of our decisions. We don't always know the full story or the exact facts, so we make assumptions to fill the gaps. They help us make sense of complex information and can serve as an important guide so we know what questions we can ask. But they limit our ability to communicate effectively.

Do any of these lines sound familiar?

- I can only assume they're going to do A…

- For the sake of this exercise, let's assume B…

- I assume they'll have access to this information through D, E, and F channels.

Assumptions can be just as harmful as they are helpful. When we fall into the trap of not challenging our assumptions and instead begin accepting them at face value, or when we fail to recognize them at all, much bigger problems can set in.

Within the first thirty minutes of these design thinking sessions, it became clear that even when we believe we're being open to information, myself included, we might not always be gathering enough of the right information to inform our communications decisions or our practices.

Time on our Side

For years, research showed that someone had seven seconds to make a first impression. That's not much time at all. But it's a lifetime compared to newer data[22] which showed the actual time it takes for someone to judge another person's character is .01 seconds.

Milliseconds.

So-fast-you-don't-even-know-it-happened seconds.

And once that very initial assumption is set, it's hard to break it. So, it's even more essential that we recognize when we're making assumptions and understand how to be intentional about listening, learning, and understanding one another to differentiate false assumptions from reality.

Mauricio Miller noticed this problem of assumptions in his work, too, and knew that a mind shift would be just as important as a system shift if we were going to be effective in reimagining the social service sector. Slack's Stewart Butterfield did, too.

> Reflect on the assumptions you make about the people you meet or the policies or practices that show up throughout the course of your day.

Take time to recognize your assumptions as you make them, and then consider how they might be wrong, ill-informed, or worth examining further. Then, think about how those assumptions might affect how you communicate, show up, and make decisions in your day-to-day work environment.

Ashton Lattimore, editor-in-chief of Prism, an independent nonprofit newsroom led by journalists of color, found herself recently in a similar situation. She examined standard practices and wondered what could happen if she dug into a new way of work—if she challenged the assumptions of a traditional newsroom. She shared what she learned with me in 2021 on the *Mission Forward* podcast.[23]

"We understand that not everyone in our readership exists within the same spaces. So, we've learned to be thoughtful about not assuming knowledge of acronyms or certain terms because we want to make sure that we are writing in a way that's open to everyone. We've also been thinking deeply about who is at the center of our stories. We recognize our responsibility as communicators to be careful about who we assume is the protagonist of a story about abortion, police violence, or voting rights. Understanding where we put our lens and not defaulting to the norm of treating power as the protagonist has been an essential shift to how we communicate."

Tips for Challenging Assumptions in Your Communication Practices

Drawing from Ashton's insights, here are three more ways you can challenge your assumptions and help to keep them in check.

How well do you listen?

As in listening without simultaneously forming a response in your mind. In our Mission Partners' Design Thinking Day sessions, we always practice the radical listening exercise outlined at the beginning of this book. For sixty seconds, participants gaze at their partners, learning one another's faces and staying connected to one another's eyes. Then, we repeat the exercise, but each person has sixty seconds to talk. And every time, something interesting happened—the room softened, the relationships deepened, and people began seeing each other in new ways, noticing little details they hadn't noticed before. Assumptions we had made about one another in those first few seconds of meeting melted away.

If you're the curator of content for your organization, where are you sourcing your news?

The easy assumption is that the sources we pull from give us a well-rounded picture of the situation. But what stories could we be missing? Are your sources the same sources week after week, or do you challenge yourself to go beyond the traditional news set? How often do you reach into your community to request news for future editions? How often do you explore the news within the outer rings of your audience set—beyond your primary audience and into your secondary and tertiary audience—to see how the conversations and news differ?

What are the things you mean to know but keep assuming you've figured out?

In an episode of *This American Life*,[24] David Kestenbaum spoke with producer Diane Wu about her list of things she "means to know." It made me think of all the things I mean to know but have not explored enough to understand fully. So, I started a list too. And while right now, the list seems to grow faster than I can check things off, it's become a great exercise in intentionally learning and breaking my own assumptions. There's little we can do about first impressions. Our brains are hardwired to fill gaps of information with assumptions, and that won't soon change. But what we do with the seconds, minutes, and hours that follow makes all the difference in this world.

BOTTOM LINE: Assumptions can have a significant and lasting influence on how you communicate, show up, and make decisions in your day-to-day work environment. Take time to recognize your assumptions as you make them, and then consider how they might be wrong, ill-informed, or worth examining further.

Chapter 18

Spotting False Urgency

"Time is what we want most,
but what we use worst."

WILLIAM PENN

I'm a runner. Not an overly accomplished one, but a runner, just the same. It's part of my identity, to the point where if I were asked to introduce myself, my affinity for running would likely show up in the first few minutes of our conversation.

However, I don't need to have ever run a race, let alone a lap around the block, to know that if you jump off the starting block at breakneck speed, you're not going to feel good at the finish.

That **race to the finish**. Even if you've never put on a pair of running shoes, I think you probably know the feeling. It shows up so often in our daily routines. The race to finish the campaign concept, the race to develop the event materials, and the race to see results. For a long time, I assumed this was just how PR professionals operated, at a pace that is entirely unrealistic at best and terribly unhealthy at worst.

Why, then, is urgency so steeped in our everyday work? One might say, "You need to have an urgency for the work if you're going to manage a crisis effectively," or "The issues are so important; how can we stand a chance at addressing them without urgency?"

In some cases, they're right. But here's the thing. There's a time and place for breakneck speed. Maybe you're closing in on new voting rights or climate change legislation and need supporting materials to help drive the case home. Maybe you're creating an experience that supports community-led innovation. Those seem like good reasons for urgency. But beware of the teams and leaders who see urgency as a daily standard and essential to individual success.

It took me years before I was ready to say to a client or a boss, "Hold on for a moment and let's talk about that timeline." Because, honestly, operating in urgency belittles strategy, despite what the experts will say.

A well-documented and defined dominant cultural norm,[25] urgency can perpetuate power imbalances. It can limit your ability to engage multiple perspectives and restrict any meaningful rest or reflection. Employing urgency effectively requires the ability to also practice stillness. Stillness supports the ability to scan the landscape, see the big picture, and strategically plan your steps before racing to the finish.

Best-selling author, Harvard professor, and change management expert John Kotter took urgency head-on in his book, A Sense of Urgency,[26] in which he made it abundantly clear that "urgency is not busyness or franticness." However, this is often how it shows up in our workplaces—a frenetic pace that leads to wasted time, wasted resources, frustrated teams and burned-out employees. On the flip side, Kotter argues that when used effectively, urgency is continual attention to the changing landscape within a company and on the outside. It is a commitment to discern what is important and to work on what really matters.

False urgency is not that. False urgency is just frenetic activity. Communicators for change know how to spot and disrupt false urgency and keep their teams focused on what matters.

Reflect on the pace you tend to keep. Does it feel comfortable? Sustainable? Enjoyable? Do you let your breakneck speed dictate the speed of those around you? Think about how a sense of urgency might contribute to your work. And then ask, if this is how we operate from a place of urgency, what remarkable impact could we have if we slowed it down for a bit?

> **BOTTOM LINE:** False urgency is a very real and very common issue in workplaces of all kinds and all sizes. False urgency is rooted in anxiety and leads to unproductive activity far more than it leads to productive results. False urgency causes burnout and unnecessary crises. Consider if you are perpetuating false urgency in your management approach, and please—on behalf of everyone who works with you—quit it.

Chapter 19

Breaking Like-Mindedness

"It is not our differences that divide us.
It is our inability to recognize, accept,
and celebrate those differences."

AUDRE LORDE

I used to think that a secret to success was surrounding myself with like-minded people. Surely, those who thought similarly to me and who had taken similar education or career paths would be my best sources of insight and information, right? Well, I thought I was right until I knew it was wrong.

It started with a class I took, hosted by CommonHealth ACTION, in which I was forced to examine a list of ten people I trust the most. No relatives, just peers, mentors, and friends, could be on the list. What I found shocked me. Nearly all ten people on my identified list looked like me. They held similar levels of education. They had similar political beliefs. They were from similar socioeconomic backgrounds. The lack of diversity floored me. And once I saw it, I vowed to do something about it.

That experiment with CommonHealth ACTION resurfaced for me while reading Bill Bishop and Robert Cushing's book, *The Big Sort: Why the Clustering of Like-Minded America is Tearing us Apart.*[27] The book uses groundbreaking research to explore how Americans have unintentionally sorted themselves into increasingly homogeneous neighborhoods, choosing to live near those who share similar beliefs, backgrounds, and socioeconomic status. It's to be expected—people naturally congregate with those like them. But, as stated in the book, "We are living with the consequences of this segregation by way of life—pockets of like-minded citizens that have become so ideologically inbred that we don't know 'those people' on the other side of the political divide who often live just a few miles away."

Hearkening back to Dr. Maya Angelou's words, if we know better, we must do better, especially regarding the dangers of groupthink. When we surround ourselves with people who tell us what we want to hear and believe what we do, it's effortless to accept that something is true because enough people around us *say* it's true. So, instead of wrestling with hard questions, or challenging norms, we simply settle for answers without ever questioning them.

NOTE: *Revisit Chapter 6 and re-read my story about the foundation presidents to see this point in action.*

Whether we like it or not, we all tend to believe that our opinions are well-informed and valid, even though we often don't know why we think the way we do. It's simply easier to believe what we want or have always believed. But there's no knowledge or power in that. Instead, work hard to listen and to understand *beyond* what you believe. Then, see if your opinion still stands.

Let's consider storytelling.

Social science research shows that you get someone to feel through story. As Lisa Cron shares in her book *Wired for Story*, "It's key to who we are. It's literally how our minds are wired to understand." For those who are religious, we know that the stories captured in holy books have kept generations engaged in their family's religion. And for those who have letters from parents or grandparents, we know the power of passing down stories to understand who we are and where we came from. Stories are a way for people to stay connected to their roots. Stories start movements and lead to change.

What if we've not only been passing down those stories but also the beliefs that come with them?

In politics, philanthropy, or professional settings, it's common to hear what we need to hear and conveniently disregard the rest. In fact, a study[28] published by the American Psychological Association confirms this idea as it found that people were *twice as likely* to select the information that supported their own point of view rather than consider an opposing idea.

This exact issue led me to write about the troubles of like-mindedness and why Mission Partners began hosting workshops on bridging cultural and communications gaps in and out of the workplace. It's why we train teams to build healthy, inclusive, and conscious work environments and why we've seen a significant increase in requests to conduct perception research.

What's interesting is that organizations aren't necessarily calling us to ask for perception research. They're calling because they want to understand why their donations are dwindling, why their membership numbers are falling, and why their subscribers are leaving. Sound like a question you've wondered, too?

The reality is, in nearly every case, at some point, the organization simply stopped listening. They began hearing only what they wanted to hear. They got caught in a web of like-mindedness.

Breaking a like-minded mentality won't happen overnight, and it won't happen without some uncomfortable experiences. But, as Albert Einstein said, "We cannot solve our problems with the same thinking we used to create them." And with the problems in our world today, there's no better time than right now to start thinking differently.

The good news is like-mindedness can be disrupted through intentional listening.

Intentional listening starts with awareness. Once you recognize when you've become surrounded by your own point of view, you know it's time for a change. Clear signs that you've entered a like-minded state include when everyone has the same opinion, mindset, and worldview or when no one offers feedback on your strategies or thoughts for improving your communication because everyone shares the same headspace. The best thing to do is poke your head up, look around, and see how you can get some fresh perspectives.

At Mission Partners, our process for breaking like-mindedness is called perception research. Before an organization releases a new brand or program, we work with them to stress test the message with people across the community, most of whom have not been at the table for any of the strategy work. We seek fresh, unfiltered opinions and insights on what works and what doesn't to ensure we are gathering insights from the widest range of audiences and perspectives. Not only can this process support an organization in hearing what it needs to hear, but it can also deliver the outside view essential for building a truly connected and authentic brand.

Tips for Breaking Like-Mindedness

Use these guiding questions to measure your like-mindedness quotient.

Examine your peer group. Take on the trust experiment yourself. Are your personal and professional circles similar to yours in their thinking and lifestyles? Do you challenge one another? How would someone in your peer group or work group react if you challenged their thinking? If those challenging conversations aren't happening often, perhaps it is time to widen your circle.

Vary your listening habits. Instead of listening to the same morning news program every day, consider trying something completely different. See what you can learn when you simply listen to a different perspective.

Go one level deeper. Take one topic you hear about today on the news or in your peer group and go deeper. Force yourself to look at both sides of the issue and try to understand what might be going on with those who think differently than you. You don't have to agree with what you learn. The point is open-heartedly learning about people's thoughts on an issue from a different perspective.

Examine how you use social media platforms. Examine the list of people and organizations you're following. Do they all generally think like you? Consider expanding who you're following to get a wider range of coverage, and intentionally follow individuals and groups outside of your comfort zone to help you think differently and see issues from another point of view.

The hard part for many organizations is to understand that we're *not* designing for ourselves, just as we hope we're not communicating to ourselves. In what ways can you better and more deeply connect with your audience?

BOTTOM LINE: Our daily lives are busy, and our task lists are endless. The notion of observing our own storytelling practices doesn't always seem feasible. But, to get to the heart of your best stories, give yourself some extra time to observe this week. Pay attention to how others receive your communications, and if like-mindedness is getting in the way of your full communications potential.

Chapter 20

Looking Between the Lines

"Anyone can play the notes.
Music is what goes on
in between the notes."

ISAAC STERN

Years ago, my dear friend and mentor Don Foley shared a story about Isaac Stern that I've never let go of. The great violinist (1920–2001) was often asked why the music sounded so different when Isaac played it on his violin versus when others followed the same song sheet.

"Anyone can play the notes," he would tell students; "Music is what goes on in between the notes."

As I've since learned, Stern wasn't alone in believing this concept. Composers and musicians throughout time, from Mozart to Claude Debussy and Miles Davis, have all shared similar sentiments—if not always with the same words, including Mozart, who said, "The music is not in the notes, but in the silence between."

I often consider this "space between" concept when working on a piece of persuasive writing or collaborating with my colleagues on a design project. Just as many music composers have found, it's not the complexity of the words or design that make a message come to life, but just the opposite—the strategic simplicity of a message can give deeper meaning to the words.

Here's a story to make it real.

Andy Miller is the best editor I've ever known. A "newspaper guy" at heart, he served for two decades as Washington correspondent for *The Kansas City Star* before moving into public affairs, where my path luckily crossed his in early 2002 at Prism Public Affairs.

Andy wrote the most incredible op-eds and speeches, and he'd do it in a matter of hours. I remember Andy stealing away to his office mid-morning, and by lunch, he'd have a solid draft ready for client review. But it wasn't the speed that impressed me—it was how he made the most of his words.

Andy thought about the space between, too, but from a different perspective. He'd say, "It's far easier to write a long-form essay than a six-hundred-word op-ed because when we have space, we'll always find ways to fill it. But if you can deliver a short-form, get-to-the-point message without any filler copy, you've made your words work for you."

Whether composing music or messages or the structure of our days, the space—and how we choose to use it—matters. Rather than finding ways to fill it, consider what might happen if you pulled back to only the essentials. Let most of your message fall to the editing room floor, and you'll see that what remains is not so different from what Stern and many others loved about the space between the notes. Here is where you find the heart of what matters most.

BOTTOM LINE: What would happen if you took a fresh look at some of your communications from recent years? What would happen if you challenged some of the default ways you engage and present stories or connect with your colleagues? Set aside expected or desired outcomes. Consider this process as a way to gain a new perspective. Examine your work and reflect on how you presently communicate; what you learn may help you adjust the process to be more inclusive in the future.

Part Two

Be the Leader We Need

Chapter 21

How to Be

"If you don't have a target,
you'll miss it every time."

PETER DIAMANDIS

Have you ever had one of those moments, maybe after a big presentation or an important conversation with a loved one, when you've wondered, *did that go okay?*

The desire to be heard, understood, and maybe even remembered—we all want that on some level. But even for the most confident people in the world, the anxiety-producing feeling of wondering *did my message make it through* is universal.

Take it from Oprah Winfrey.

Between 1986 and 2011—a twenty-five-year span—Oprah interviewed more than 37,000 people on her talk show, *The Oprah Winfrey Show*. She interviewed some of the most famous people in the world and some lesser-known people who became famous after they sat next to her in the studio.

As every single one of those 37,000 interviews concluded, the first question, often whispered, was always the same:

Did that go okay?

In one form or another, everyone just wants to be seen and heard—but even the most confident of storytellers doubt their effectiveness.

Since realizing that, Winfrey has made a conscious effort to validate the people she interacts with day to day. She has learned to be more present in every interaction, realizing how important it is to acknowledge the courage in every story she hears.

It's a good reminder to acknowledge and thank the people who help make us courageous communicators. The people who validate our stories and listen when it feels like no one else is. The people who have answered "Yes, it was great" when you've asked, "Did that go okay?"

It's an equally important reminder to be that sounding board and support system for others.

I was reminded of Oprah's a-ha moment while listening to an episode of the Hidden Brain[29] podcast, in which Shankar Vedantam interviewed psychologist Harry Reis. The pair discussed the role of empathy in managing through conflict, noting that even when conflicts don't get resolved, the interactions are less harmful to relationships when people feel like they've been *heard and understood*.

There's no escaping it. We all want to be seen and heard.

But getting there? It involves courage. The courage to share who I really am and the courage to listen to who you really are. Whether we have the perfect words or not.

> **BOTTOM LINE:** There is a vulnerability in letting someone see and hear us, but in the end, it's also what we want most. So, if you're wondering how to get people to see and hear more from you, lean into that vulnerability. Consider what walls you've put up around you and try taking them down, if just a bit. I suspect your message might resonate even more as a result.

How Do I Say This?

Similar to Oprah's story, there's a little phrase I've been asked more than any other in my twenty years as a social impact communications consultant, "How do I say this?"

Whether whispered to me by the leader of a global non-profit or discretely asked by the founders of a successful, venture-backed startup, I've had some of the best public communicators confide in me that they struggle to communicate.

Here's the essential nuance. Rarely do I hear leaders express challenges about technical communication—about their work, product, or business model. The bigger challenge often lies squarely in one place, interpersonal communications.

When I started in the field of social impact communications in the early 2000s, I didn't yet understand the deep connection between the personal communications skills of a leader and an organization's overall success. Only much later, upon reflection, did I realize just how strong the connection is.

I connected these dots in early 2020 as employers grappled with the pandemic and renewed calls for racial justice. The global workforce focused on leadership, taking notice of leaders who prioritized people first. And I observed something, too: some leaders rose to the moment while many others struggled mightily. Upon closer inspection, the ones who struggled to find their words were often the same ones getting harsh pushback from their employees and seeing greater numbers of unexplained resignations.

While outliers always exist, I believe most organizations want to build workplaces that work for everyone. But when it comes to issues of diversity, equity, inclusion, and belonging, a near-daily stream of intentions gone awry seems present. Sometimes, these commitments are performative, and those efforts are doomed from the start. But other times, the intention gets lost in the delivery. How we communicate gets in the way of what we're trying to communicate, which makes any well-intentioned communications go wrong.

It's not what you say; it's *how you say it*. How you present your information matters to your employees, teams, and your long-term organizational success.

After these twenty years, it's never been clearer. What you say when the spotlight isn't on you is just as important, if not more so, as what you say when the room is packed. How you act on your values as a leader is just as important as the values themselves. But getting to a place where you can realize your maximum potential as a leader and a communicator comes down to this one factor—you.

As you explore the next section of the book, consider these prompts.

THINK ABOUT THIS. How do you currently show your commitment to issues and causes that you care most about? Would someone meeting you for the first time know anything about your passion areas?

WRITE THIS DOWN. How could you ensure that your values appear more actively in everyday actions and decision-making?

Chapter 22

What Do You Stand For?

"We have talked enough; but we have
not listened. And by not listening we
have failed to concede the immense
complexity of our society—and thus the
great gaps between ourselves and those
with whom we seek understanding."

WILLIAM H. WHYTE

What do you stand for?

It's a question that often comes up in our work, particularly when guiding organizations in delivering their
most compelling messages. After years of working with
mission-driven organizations, I know that articulating an
organization's belief is central to having others believe in it.

So, what do you stand for?

As introduced in Chapter 9, this is not an easy question
to answer. Most have a much easier time answering, "What
are you against?" even though the answer to the first question is at the heart of your organization's purpose and values.
But getting to that place of clarity and then needing to stick

with the answer—it's easier said than done, particularly when economics are at play.

For many individuals and organizations, committing to a clear, well-stated and understood-by-all purpose is no small task. Once that purpose is clear, however, as we saw in the Slack case study, then other business decisions start to fall into place.

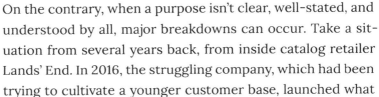

On the contrary, when a purpose isn't clear, well-stated, and understood by all, major breakdowns can occur. Take a situation from several years back, from inside catalog retailer Lands' End. In 2016, the struggling company, which had been trying to cultivate a younger customer base, launched what it called the Legend Series[30] to feature individuals who have "...made a difference in both their respective industries and the world at large."

The first interview in the series featured Gloria Steinem, highlighting her work to pass the Equal Rights Amendment. The interview further explored challenges for women in the workplace, the renewed drive for an equal rights amendment, and Steinem's path through life.

Hours after the catalog and the corresponding interview went live, a flood of criticism prompted the clothing company to remove all references to Steinem from its website and subsequently issued the following statement.

"We understand that some of our customers were offended by the inclusion of an interview in a recent catalog with Gloria Steinem on her quest for women's equality. We thought it was a good idea and we heard from our customers that, for different reasons, it wasn't. For that, we apologize.

Our goal was to feature individuals with different interests and backgrounds that have made a difference for our new Legends Series, not to take any political or religious stance."

That, however, is not where it ended. A second wave of criticism erupted from another set of angry customers who called out the organization's inability to defend its position and called their decision an insult to women's rights. A debate soon erupted on the Lands' End Facebook page.

To think this could have all been avoided if the leadership at Land's End had taken more time to figure out who they were and what they stood for before taking on what they should have known could be a controversial choice for the first interview. Their mistake wasn't in who they chose as the honoree; it was in their failure to anticipate the likely reaction. The company rushed right into the center of two equally strong opinions with no preparation and little ground of their own to stand on.

As Jay Livingston, chair of the sociology department at Montclair State University, commented, "Their dilemma on Steinem reflects their dilemma on clothing and clientele. Lands' End wants to attract younger shoppers, who lean toward the pro-choice side, but not lose their older customers, who lean in the opposite direction."[31]

I tend to think many of us run our organizations like we run our bodies. We have the best intentions to make them operate at their highest levels, but when it comes to strengthening our core, many of us get distracted along the way. Because, just like our bodies, facing our places of greatest weakness can feel like our highest priority, just until it becomes our most daunting task.

Here's how I've seen it play out:

- A nonprofit adopts a bold strategic plan and commits to a focused set of activities. But six months in, their focus has been distracted by other pressing activities, and their core, once at its strongest, is weakened.

- A foundation makes a bold commitment to shift resources to under-invested communities but still relies on the same tools for their grantmaking, reverting to their traditions. Their core philosophy, once strong, is weakened using old tools.

Finding our core and sticking to it is one of the challenging but essential tasks we face as leaders. But here's the thing, if our bodies are built on a shaky core, our lives will suffer as a result. It's no different for our organizations. Build a house on an unstable foundation, and you're bound to have bigger problems down the road.

So, if our core is essential to long-term health, then maybe it's time to think about your work through this lens:

- **What will it take to strengthen my core?**

  What is central to your approach as a business, a team, and a leader? What values do you hold dear, and what is essential to protect and preserve always? In other words, what would you do tomorrow, and the day after that, even if you didn't have the resources to do it? The answers will help you refocus on your core.

- **And what is a distraction from my core?**

    Who or what are you not? What will you never become? What will we refuse to do, even if you were handed $100M to expand your results? Knowing your organization and yourself is essential to staying focused on who you are.

As communicators, we present to the world not just empty words or ideas but words and ideas baked in beliefs. For the strongest, clearest, and most compelling words to come through, we need to know what we believe in. We need to know what we hold sacred. We need to know undeniably and without question who we are and who we are not. What we will do and what we will never do. Jim Knight, executive director of Jubilee Housing, understands this well.

Jubilee Housing's Core: Justice Housing

Jim Knight has led Jubilee Housing as its president and CEO since 2002, guiding strategic direction for the organization's mission and vision. He also spearheaded the launch of the Justice Housing Partners Fund, an impact investing fund to support affordable housing in Washington, DC. He helped establish the Platform of Hope, working with families in Adams Morgan, a neighborhood of Washington, DC, and a collective impact initiative, working with partners to establish city-wide housing and services for residents returning from incarceration.

Jubilee supports about one thousand people each year, from infants to older adults. Jim's mission is to ensure that each and every person has access to housing that is safe and high quality. To him, it's a matter of justice.

Here's how he described it on an episode of the *Mission Forward* podcast:[32]

"We need to have neighborhoods that are socially and economically diverse. That is sacred to our community. As the equity and inclusion movement has regained our attention, cities and neighborhoods can't be equitable if they're not inclusive. So, [the framework of] Justice Housing helps both those individuals who may not otherwise have a safe place to be. It also helps everyone by keeping us diverse and inclusive. Bottom line, if we found ourselves no longer leading through our commitment to this community—to its history, its residents, and its deep diversity, in favor of donor dollars, big checks, or big opportunities beyond our neighborhood lines, we'd have lost our way."

Like Jim Knight and Jubilee Housing, knowing your own values and virtues can guide you and steer you through business, but more importantly, through life—through those most vexing of challenges and the most challenging of times. Knowing who we are and who we are not can help us determine what we say yes and no to, and it can help chart our respective paths through life. Most importantly, knowing what we value and what we do not can keep us anchored.

So, ask yourself. Who are you? And who are you not? What are the values that define you? And what would you do differently if you lived fully through those values?

BOTTOM LINE: We can't have it all. We can't have clear values and then decide sometimes we'll compromise them. It comes down to clearly and definitively knowing who you are and who you are not at your core.

Chapter 23

Seeking Common Ground

"All of us share this world for but a brief
moment in time. The question is whether
we spend that time focused on what
pushes us apart, or whether we commit
ourselves to to find common ground."

Not too long ago, I was working with a national advocacy
organization that had recently completed a merger. On
paper, these two organizations coming together was a brilliant idea. Each team had a strong track record of success,
and a merger meant they could significantly impact an issue
of growing global importance.

While the merger provided a necessary influx of resources
and momentum for their rapidly growing work, the newly
formed organization came to me experiencing a palpable
sense of loss.

The new organization's leaders largely agreed with one
another, but they were out of sync on the how and the why of
the work. They interpreted their work's purpose differently,

which caused unexpected levels of friction across all parts of the newly expanded team. What once looked like a brilliant idea now felt like a breaking point for several senior staff members.

"This was supposed to be a good move for everyone involved. It was supposed to build efficiency and increase resources, but instead, it feels like we're constantly waging uphill battles and not making any progress at all on our goals."

This is what my friend Dr. Kisha Brown likes to call "digging through rocks with spoons." A clear vision and focus for success once existed but fell apart in implementation without the appropriate tools or support to navigate through the change. Without the right communications support to guide people through the transition, the piles of rocks seemed endless.

And so, they came to me with a question. Would this friction point signal the end of their efforts, or could they get this merger back on track? It's a big question with a relatively simple answer.

There's a big difference between a concept on paper and a concept in practice. A merger can look beautiful in theory. It can appear to be the perfect solution to an organization's most pressing issues. But introduce the dynamics of people into that perfect model, and you're sure to have challenges that weren't visible in a two-dimensional view.

At Mission Partners, we invest time exploring and examining what works in moving a mission forward. We dig deep into the barriers that prevent brands from achieving their full potential. And through this work, we always find the same factor at play—as mentioned in Chapter 3—the human factor.

Rather than question if the merger was a good idea or write it off as a failure, these moments of transition can serve as the perfect opportunity for a guided reset. This discomfort prompts a fresh look at an organization's mission, vision, and values set. It creates an intentional opportunity to explore with fresh eyes how the grounding beliefs of any organization play out in its day-to-day operations, management, and culture.

When committed to and communicated regularly, shared values can provide a framework to guide business decisions. Shared values bring consistency, and shared values foster high-impact teams and organizations. If values are misaligned, as they were when these organizations first came to us, you can also expect to see other parts of the organization misaligned.

If you want to get more out of your team or organization and wonder what role values alignment could play, ask yourself this set of guiding questions:

- **What is core and sacred to your work?** What are the values that drive you and help clarify why your organization exists in the world?

- **If asked, would your Board and/or leadership team have a similar answer?**

- **What is most different in how you understand or interpret your core values?**

- **How have those values changed or shifted over time?** And are there opportunities to align the team more deeply around a core set of shared values?

Then, manifest it. Imagine what it would look like to fully live into those values. What would need to change about your current operations? Your current practices? Your current staff dynamics and team makeup? What would change about how you show up in the work?

This is not an activity for the faint of heart and can't be done in the span of a half-day leadership retreat. But if you commit to starting this exploration and contemplate it over the coming months, I guarantee that by the end of the process, you will have a new clarity of purpose, a deeper understanding of your organization's why, and a more focused path for the future.

By articulating, testing, and practically applying a values set across an organization, not only can you strengthen—or reset, if needed—a team dynamic, but you can advance a mission in ways never thought possible on a sheet of paper.

BOTTOM LINE: If you wonder why your team or organization isn't performing as expected or why that concept on paper just isn't scaling as it should, take a pause and check on the connection. See if the forces powering the work are coordinated and if the human dynamics are values-aligned. If they're not, you could be ready for a reset.

Chapter 24

People First

"No one cares how much you know,
until they know how much you care."

THEODORE ROOSEVELT

Several years ago, a young employee had difficulty concentrating at work. While it was clear she was struggling to connect with her peers and meet certain deadlines, she was also noticeably uncomfortable sharing details of her struggle.

Rather than scold her for missing deadlines—my first inclination—I took a deep breath and asked her to join me for a walk. We found a little table at an outdoor café and talked about seemingly inconsequential matters first. Then she shared that her grandmother was ill. She was having difficulty thinking about anything other than how she would get back home to visit with her. She was a new employee and hadn't yet worked up the vacation time to step away.

As she talked, I no longer saw her as a new employee causing issues among the team but as a young person feeling overwhelmed by the illness of someone very special to her. I suggested she take the rest of the week off to be with her family, knowing that we would manage her assignments for the remainder of the week.

Looking back, it was such a small gesture, but it deeply and positively changed our relationship and her future performance. It was also my light bulb moment to the power of listening and learning from my employees and the importance of leading with empathy in the workplace. As is often attributed to Theodore Roosevelt, "Nobody cares how much you know until they know how much you care."

Empathy is defined in many ways, but I understand it as the ability to see the world through another's eyes. The importance of empathy has long been understood among educators, parents, and physicians, but only recently has it emerged among the shortlist of required skills for successful CEOs. Empathy is an essential tool for business success, directly correlating to growth, productivity, and earnings per employee.

When you allow yourself to see situations from another's perspective, you create an environment for employees and peers to feel safe with failures or to ask for support when challenges arise. When our leaders are empathetic—and, by extension, kind—we become more loyal to our employees and therefore work harder to do right by them. And, in this particularly divisive time, how can we be anything but kind?

Yet, according to the annual Workplace Empathy Monitor research,[33] empathy doesn't come easy. As 2017 research specifically found and has been reinforced in the research every year since, while 60 percent of employers believe their organizations are empathetic, just 24 percent of employees agree.

Many times, leaders think they are being empathetic. They think they are creating space for an understanding environment. But they don't take the time to really listen and learn from their employees.

The good news is there are some straightforward strategies to build compassionate leadership in your day-to-day activities. The following list is adapted from the teachings of Roman Krznaric and the Greater Good Science Center at UC Berkeley.

Provide experience rather than advice.

Frederique Irwin, the brilliant mind behind Her Corner,[34] used to ask members in her accelerator programs to abide by the Gestalt Language Protocol, in which individuals speak from experience rather than give advice. For instance, saying, "Here's what worked for me..." is far more effective and empathic than saying, "Here's what you should do..." or "Here's what I would do..."

Listen rather than analyze.

The person with whom you're speaking likely isn't expecting or wanting you to have the answer, nor do they want to be immediately judged or evaluated on the information they are sharing. Rather than jumping to a statement like "I think you're taking this the wrong way..." or "You're taking this too seriously..." just listen and avoid the urge to have "the right answer."

Focus on understanding rather than defending.

If an employee or peer has difficult information to share with you, give them the time and space to share without immediately jumping to your own defense. It is far more effective to let someone explain what is bothering them and then to calmly enter the conversation without rushing to give your side of the story—even if you believe you are right.

Give the person speaking your full attention.
Offer the person in front of you your sole focus. Multitasking, while a great skill, is not appropriate when working empathically. Instead, practice active listening. Tune into what your conversation partner is saying without interruption. Pay careful attention to their body language and facial expressions and periodically repeat back to them what you think they're trying to say to make sure you understand them accurately. The next time you're in conversation and actively listening, focus on the color of your conversation partner's eyes. Tune in to them fully, and you'll likely find that you will hear them better than you have in the past.

Look for commonalities.
Approach your day knowing that you have at least one thing in common with every person you interact with—on the train, in the coffee shop, and at work. When interacting with people who seem to be different from you, look for sources of commonality and shared experience. Maybe you're both fans of the same sports team, or you both know what it's like to lose a loved one. Seeing your shared identity[35] can help you overcome fear and distrust and promote empathy and cooperation.

Share in other people's joy.
Empathy is not just about commiserating; it can also be experienced in response to positive emotions such as happiness and pride. If you hear someone else sharing good news or celebrating a special moment at work, step away from your computer, and express your enthusiasm for their good news.

Moments like this take mere seconds, but they are essential for the well-being of a relationship.

And finally, between comfortable communication and uncomfortable, always choose uncomfortable. It makes the product better.

> **BOTTOM LINE:** There will always be more to people's stories than they let on. Start every day from a place of compassion and an understanding that it's okay not to know all the answers. And, in taking the time to understand others, they'll likely take time to understand you better, too.

Chapter 25

The Team Can See You Now

"Take the long way.
Do the hard work, consistently
and with generosity and transparency.
And then you won't waste time doing it over."

SETH GODIN

At all levels of work, employees expect broader levels of humanity, understanding, and honesty from their leaders. This requires leaders to be engaged, committed, and genuine in their thoughts and actions. For many leaders, that's easier said than done, especially as they feel the spotlight's bright lights on them today more than ever.

Neil Patel, New York Times best-selling author, believes[36] that being authentic means "...staying true to who you are, what you do, and who you serve." This human element "...continually creates value, benefits your customers and improves your business."

Marketing speak aside, being authentic also involves a level of integrity that includes honesty and transparency.

Communicating authentically and transparently can help employees feel like they are part of something bigger. It can invite your colleagues to be a part of your business and its vision, which often translates into more loyal team members. But too much—or not enough—of anything can backfire on your business and on you as the leader. Finding the right balance is essential and can be best determined by asking employees regularly for feedback to inform your actions as a leader.

Being a communicator for change requires also being transparent and purposeful in your words and actions. Being transparent doesn't mean you need to share every last detail of the business with your employees, but it does mean being honest and open when communicating with stakeholders about matters related to the business.

Let's talk about what it looks like to be effectively transparent and what it looks like to take transparency too far.

To do that, let's head back to the Slack/Next Chapter partnership.

In 2018, when the executive team of Slack was setting in motion their Next Chapter pilot program, designed to shift perceptions about the potential of people who have been incarcerated and to generate new opportunities in skilled, long-term employment in the technology sector for re-entering individuals, they knew transparency would be essential to their success.

The team needed to create a safe space for employees and for the apprentices—some would be entering the workforce for the first time. So Slack also invested resources in educating employees through regular office hours and town hall meetings. Slack leadership convened two all-staff meetings around criminal justice, held office hours for employees to voice concerns, and created opportunities for employees to visit San Quentin. Since that first visit in 2016, more than two hundred Slack employees have visited San Quentin and The Last Mile program. These visits to San Quentin were cited by nearly all employees who attended as the single most important moment in building buy-in for the program.

As Dawn Sharifan, former Senior Vice President of People, noted, "After that shared experience, we started to think about what the program could look like, how we would set criteria for eligibility, and what roles the apprentices could play within the company. We thought through how to run background checks and how to balance the apprenticeship with safety and security commitments we had made to our customers to ensure the program had every chance at success."

Building meaningful transparency means letting employees into your business initiatives in meaningful ways, helping them build knowledge, understanding and value while creating an open dialogue to share concerns and questions.

To situate your organization for the best possible outcomes, I suggest the classic Stoic virtue, "It's not what happens to you, but how you react to it that matters." Simply put, you don't control what happens, but only you can control how you respond. As history has shown, often, an organization's response to a challenging moment—a pandemic or a disappointed customer—will determine whether its stakeholders view the organization in a negative or positive light in the future.

What You Say and What You Do Matters

The rules guiding today's work world are light-years different from just a decade ago. And while that change can be hard for some leaders to adapt to and rise to, we know that change itself is good. Leaders are being held accountable. But they need to act as such, which means addressing issues in the moment, even when you don't have all the answers. In recent years, I've seen executives, leadership teams, and project managers alike struggle through key decision-making moments. Where leaders were once confident in their decision-making, they now question themselves and their choices. But we all know how that story ends. When leaders don't make the decisions they need to make, their entire team feels the effect.

If you find yourself in a challenging situation, your response and talking points should express integrity, transparency, openness, accountability, and commitment. Provide as much relevant and accurate information as possible without sharing more than you can at that moment. While advantages to a cautious approach to communications under challenging situations exist, so does the great danger of not communicating quickly enough and then being perceived as unresponsive or secretive. The more rapidly and prudently you begin to communicate, the more likely you are to gain control of the communications and gain the trust of your team.

Here are a few tips if you find yourself in a similar situation.

It's okay to pause.
If you've said something you didn't intend and think you may have harmed or hurt someone in the process, it's okay to take

a pause. Think for a moment why what you said could have been harmful, even if your motivation was good.

Validate the effect.

After you've given yourself a moment of pause, validate the actual effect of your actions. You can do this by acknowledging to your peers, family, or friends that you can see how you hurt them. Try noticing aloud what you see, such as, "I can tell what I said didn't go over as intended. I want to pause here and acknowledge that."

Own your actions.

The crucial final step is to apologize for the harm that your words or actions had on someone. While it can feel hard to apologize for something we didn't mean to do, it is essential if you care about building or maintaining trust with those receiving your comments. You may not always understand why your words had such an effect, but the apology matters. Try this, "I want to apologize for the harm I caused by my comment. I intended to raise the issue as I've experienced it, but I poorly chose to compare my circumstances with yours. I am sorry."

> **BOTTOM LINE:** Transparency is a throwaway term unless you're actually practicing it. Delivering on what you say you'll do is the ground floor for building trust. If you've taken the time to develop shared values and then choose not to live through them, expect to find yourself in the spotlight for all the wrong reasons.

Part Three

From Here
to Where?

Chapter 26

Decision Points

"All stories have a curious and even dangerous power. They are manifestations of truth—yours and mine. And truth is all at once the most wonderful yet terrifying thing in the world, which makes it nearly impossible to handle."

VERA NAZARIAN

When I was young, I loved the *Choose Your Own Adventure* book series. Each book in the set presented readers with a unique set of pathways that—based on your own choices as a reader—would determine the main character's actions and the plot's outcome. It was brilliant, really. If you didn't like the ending you chose, then you could simply head back to page one and take a different path. You could start all over again.

If only life let us do the same.

While there's no option for going back to page one in life, we face critical decision points nearly every day, some far more complex than others. Our decisions in those moments matter and, just like in a *Choose Your Own Adventure* book, can determine what happens next.

You might be choosing between one strategic priority or another, but you might also be choosing between this investment or that one. Maybe you're choosing between the career you have or the career you want. Perhaps as you're reading this, you're choosing between staying on social media or saying goodbye.

Sometimes the choice is a clear one, but sometimes that fork in the road stumps us, and we become consumed with the weight of the decision.

If you find yourself faced with similar challenges, then I've got a tool for you.

Early in the pandemic, when everything felt out of our control, our team created a tool to help guide leaders in making better, more informed decisions. It's a simple impact/risk matrix that may be helpful for you, too. The matrix offers some basic framing for how and when to make a public statement, when to consider a shift in strategy, or when to activate a crisis communications plan. Regardless of the decision, the matrix serves as a critical tool for navigating complicated fork-in-the-road moments.

A simplified version of the matrix goes like this:

- **Start with the choices in front of you and take a deep breath.** While the choices might not all be good choices, acknowledge that you do have *choices*. Choice, as I've learned, is a gift. Take stock of the choices in front of you.

- **Then, start looking more closely at each of your choices.** You can do this through a simple X/Y axis, with a high-low impact on one side and a high-low risk on the other.

- Consider which of your choices has the potential to have a high impact—helping you advance your personal or organizational purpose and goals in a meaningful way, even if it is complicated or expensive in the near term.

- On the other side, consider which choices are low impact—ones that might provide an easy, clear, or safe path forward, but their long-term impact is questionable.

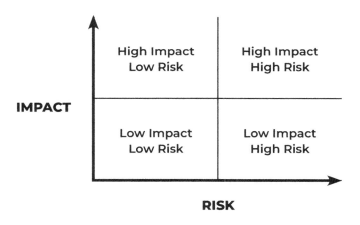

- **Consider long- and short-term risks.** Think of the long- and short-term risks associated with your high- and low-impact decision points, and plot your decisions accordingly.

- **Assess your findings.** Step back and look at what lives in your high-impact/low-risk quadrant. Whatever choice sits there may be the path calling you forward.

> **BOTTOM LINE:** Life is complicated. This is certain. And the decisions we make on any given day can determine our path forward, so making the most of them really does matter. Use this tool the next time you're faced with a fork-in-the-road moment, and remember, while you can't go back to page one, you can always progress forward. Something even better might be waiting for you in the next chapter.

Chapter 27

Gear Up

"Nothing will work unless you do."

DR. MAYA ANGELOU

When I think about gearing up, whether for a brand-new assignment or a hiking trip, I consider what I need to feel ready and equipped to take on the challenge. As we near the end of the book, it's time to see if you've got the right gear to take on the role of a communications change agent.

This book has shown you many of the skills required to employ social change in your work, community, and with your colleagues. Creating positive change requires a willingness to listen, learn, engage, and act in service of the end goal and of the people involved while reaching that end goal. And it requires practice.

The bottom line of all of this is simple. To achieve your full potential as a communicator for change, you must gear up for the responsibility of your role.

Let's take a closer look at the GEAR UP principles of social change communications:

- **Be genuine in your words and approach.** Express care and concern for stakeholders and their feelings. Listen carefully and between the words.

- **Be expressive and engaged.** Work to understand the situation from multiple perspectives, particularly those often left out of decision-making conversations.

- **Be active.** Take your role seriously. Engage with your colleagues to monitor and track your communication rather than waiting for someone to deliver feedback.

- **Be responsive to issues and requests.** Show that you care, don't just say that you care. This includes being transparent in your communications and your actions. Being transparent shows that you are willing to hold yourself accountable, and it shows that you value learning and growth. Make intentional changes when things go wrong, and communicate through failure as a way to support others in their own growth paths.

- **Update.** Don't just respond once and assume an issue is addressed. When you've been given feedback on your communications, welcome it, and then follow up, check in, and provide updates. And if you've made a misstep, own up to it and take action to fix the issue.

- **Power share.** Find ways to lift others on your team, even if that means getting yourself out of the way first. Don't control so much of the process that you lose opportunities to teach, train and celebrate team members supporting your success.

We designed the GEAR UP concept to help you get and stay equipped for the mountains and hills you may face in your own social change work.

The GEAR UP Principles:

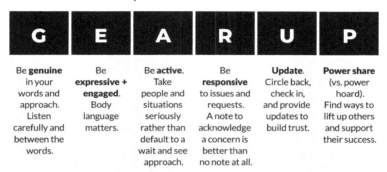

G	E	A	R	U	P
Be **genuine** in your words and approach. Listen carefully and between the words.	Be **expressive + engaged**. Body language matters.	Be **active**. Take people and situations seriously rather than default to a wait and see approach.	Be **responsive** to issues and requests. A note to acknowledge a concern is better than no note at all.	**Update**. Circle back, check in, and provide updates to build trust.	**Power share** (vs. power hoard). Find ways to lift up others and support their success.

BOTTOM LINE: Social change doesn't happen overnight, and it doesn't happen without human change. Consider your role in advancing social change—or holding it back. Own your role and use it responsibly.

Chapter 28

The Power Is Yours

"The power to question is the
basis of all human progress."

INDIRA GANDHI

What if I told you that some of our finest ideas never see the light of day because of a communications problem? Specifically, an internal communications problem.

We hold ourselves back. We tell ourselves we're not ready yet, or the time isn't right. But *what if* we took a little step forward toward our big idea each day or each week? Over time, that incremental progress can lead to big things. It just requires momentum. And maybe a few good pep talks.

Frank Luntz, a political pollster and commentator, coined the phrase, "It's not what you say; it's what people hear." That one line gets to the heart of what this book is about. Each of us has an important message we want to share with the world, but being heard relies on how we craft and deliver our message and if someone can hear what we need them to hear.

In addition to people hearing your words, a more important outcome is how your words make people feel.

As I hope you found in the pages of this book, what we do is just as important as what we say.

In communications, we often get wrapped up in getting every word right, so much so that the power of the story can get lost in the process. The most effective messages are often the ones that come from the heart.

Glinda the Good, a witch in *The Wizard of Oz*, said it best, "You've had it all along."

And you, too, have the power to take it from here.

BOTTOM LINE: Lean into the space where your passion and purpose meet—those places where you believe you can have the most significant impact on the world. And then, dig in. Hone your craft. Build a plan. Tell yourself you can.

Before you know it, bit by bit, you'll be well on your way, and you won't need to think about whether or not to get started—because you will already be on your way.

Epilogue

My journey to this book started with a question my colleague and dear friend Bridget Pooley posed to me a few years back. We were deep in the throes of thinking about how our small firm would respond in the wake of George Floyd's murder and as the racial reckoning in the United States was coming to a head. We, leaders of a small B Corporation and communications firm, were clear about one thing. We needed to do something, and we needed to make it matter.

What we'd do wasn't the question. Instead, we were focused on how far we'd go.

She said, "How far are we willing to go to challenge white supremacist norms in our work? And if we say justice matters, are we willing to go where justice requires?"

For years, we've been clear in our values at Mission Partners. We listen from the head and the heart. We regularly turn down lucrative assignments when they are not in line with our values, and we operate through a mission-locked position that business can, in fact, work for all and for the long term. But, these questions—these big, unruly, and complicated questions—about how far we could go in service of our mission would set us on a course to make our work matter on a deeper level.

Once we had the grounding tools, it didn't take us long to realize that many dominant norms—values of individualism, perfectionism, only one right way, and urgency—are present in nearly every business in Western culture. These norms were even further baked into the fabric of a communications agency such as ours.

If our objective was to strip our business of dominant norms, then we might as well close our doors and walk away. But the objective wasn't to rid our business of norms. Our objective was to ask, *what if.* What if there was another way of doing business? One that didn't compromise on our values *and* moved us toward a more just and equitable world. And *what if* we put every bit of our muscle and mind into finding the answer?

What started with a question has turned into a north star. It's not easy, and we don't always get it right, but it is core to our commitment as a B Corporation, and it has become increasingly essential for our small business.

Our company didn't set out to become a Certified B Corporation so we could market ourselves as such or to grow our company—those are both happy outcomes of a much deeper reason that led us to become B certified. Rather, we set out to achieve the B Corp Certification because we believe deeply in building better business. We appreciate knowing that the B Corp community is willing to have brave conversations about what the future of business can be rather than what the history of business has been.

But I see now, through the lens of our B Corp structure, that building a better business requires more than heart, smarts, guts, and luck. It also requires courage and a commitment to make decisions that benefit our people and our planet, even when they are not in the business owner's best interest. Those difficult decisions—that hard work—have most strengthened our business.

Being a B Corp and learning to live into our values fully means being willing to go there—wherever our employees, our communities, and our planet requires—and seeing those actions through fully. It means wholeheartedly promoting courageous leadership within our company—not because those words sound interesting, but because inherently, we know that doing so will build a better, more sustainable, and more just version of our business.

In business, as in life, shortcuts are always available. This might look like purporting the B Corp philosophy without having done the work or making broad statements about equity without digging deeply into the causes and consequences of inequities in your own workforce. But, just as shortcuts exist, so too do opportunities to examine our work more closely, opportunities to examine the process, consider the construct, and reimagine the outcome.

As you reflect on the lessons of this book, keep this in mind: every organization and every leader have many pathways available along the journey. There's never only one right way. So, let your values guide you. Without knowing what you value, you'll never know how far you can go.

If you need a thought partner along the way, I'll be here for you. Email me at carrie@missionforward.us to share what's sticking with you from this book or if there's something in your own work that's got you stewing. You can also check out my podcast, subscribe to my blog and join our community of practice over at www.MissionForward.us.

To the journey—
Carrie

Endnotes

INTRODUCTION

1 "Great Recession." Wikipedia, The Free Encyclopedia, Wikimedia Foundation, December 26, 2022. https://en.wikipedia.org/wiki/Great_Recession

2 "Public's Priorities for 2010: Economy, Jobs, Terrorism." Pew Research Center, Washington, D.C. January 5, 2010. https://www.pewresearch.org/politics/2010/01/25/publics-priorities-for-2010-economy-jobs-terrorism/

CHAPTER 1

3 MacArthur Foundation, "Maurice Lim Miller," n.d. https://www.macfound.org/fellows/class-of-2012/maurice-lim-miller.

4 In 2021, Family Independence Initiative changed its name to UpTogether, along with changes to key elements of its model. Mauricio is no longer connected to the U.S. effort and has shifted his focus to bringing the original FII model to communities across the globe. To learn more about Mauricio and to read his book, visit www.thealternativebook.org

CHAPTER 3

5 Crucial Learning, "New Study Shows People Have Never Been More Afraid to Speak Their Minds" [Press Release]. November 9, 2021. https://www.prnewswire.com/news-releases/new-study-shows-people-have-never-been-more-afraid-to-speak-their-minds-301420083.html

6 Mission Partners, "From Soft Skills to Hard Truths," May 2023. www.Mission.Partners/reports

7 Raffaella Sadun, Joseph Fuller, Stephen Hansen, and PJ Neal, "The C-Suite Skills That Matter Most." *Harvard Business Review*, September 26, 2022. https://hbr.org/2022/07/the-c-suite-skills-that-matter-most.

CHAPTER 4

8 Catalyst, "Three Quarters of Employees Say Racial Equity Policies Are Not Genuine" [Press Release]. June 21, 2022. www.catalyst.org/media-release/words-arent-enough/

9 Pozin, Ilya, "How To Engage An Increasingly Diverse Consumer Market." *Forbes*, November 9, 2015. https://www.forbes.com/sites/ilyapozin/2015/11/09/how-to-engage-an-increasingly-diverse-consumer-market.

CHAPTER 6

10 The Last Mile has become one of the most requested prison education programs in the United States. To learn more or support their work, visit www.thelastmile.org

11 Slack, "Slack for Good." Slack, n.d. https://www.slack.com/about/slack-for-good.

12 Slack, "A Blueprint for Change," August 2019. https://slackhq.com/dotcom/dotcom/wp-content/uploads/sites/6/2019/08/A-Blueprint-for-Change.pdf

CHAPTER 7
13 Raillan Brooks, "'He,' 'She,' 'They' and Us," *The New York Times*, April 5, 2017. https://www.nytimes.com/2017/04/05/insider/reporting-limits-of-language-transgender-genderneutral-pronouns.html
14 Sam Morales, "Tips for Avoiding Ableist Language and Terms — IndieSpace." IndieSpace, July 27, 2022. https://www.indiespace.org/updates/disability-pride-awareness-month-the-language-and-terms-we-use.

CHAPTER 8
15 Tim Brown, "Design Thinking." *Harvard Business Review*, October 22, 2020, from the Magazine June 2008. https://hbr.org/2008/06/design-thinking.
16 Clara Miller, "Building a Foundation for the 21st Century: Part I—On Full Philanthropic Engagement," *Nonprofit Quarterly*, June 8, 2016. https://nonprofitquarterly.org/building-a-foundation-for-the-21st-century-part-i-on-full-philanthropic-engagement/
17 The *Mission Forward* podcast, "Rewriting the Future of a Free and Just Press with Alicia Bell," July 12, 2021. https://www.missionforward.us/episodes/rewriting-the-future-of-a-free-and-just-press-with-media-2070s-alicia-bell

CHAPTER 12
18 Mission Partners' Equity Impact Analysis Tool is inspired by a tool developed by the Race Matters Institute.

CHAPTER 13
19 Krista Tippett, "Trabian Shorters, A Cognitive Skill to Magnify Humanity," *On Being*, February 3, 2022. https://onbeing.org/programs/trabian-shorters-a-cognitive-skill-to-magnify-humanity/

CHAPTER 16
20 Philip Lewis, @Phil_Lewis_ March 13, 2022. Here's the clip of Jane Campion's speech #CriticsChoiceAwards [TWEET] "Twitter" https://twitter.com/Phil_Lewis_/status/1503206213579853826
21 Ronald Johnson, "Save Lives: End the HIV Stigma," CNN.com, July 19, 2012. https://www.cnn.com/2012/07/19/opinion/johnson-hiv-stigma/index.html

CHAPTER 17
22 Simon Makin, "We accurately weigh up a person's character in 0.1 seconds," *New Scientist*, September 28, 2016. https://www.newscientist.com/article/mg23130930-500-we-accurately-weigh-up-a-persons-character-in-01-seconds
23 The *Mission Forward* podcast, "Communicating the Counter Narrative with Ashton Lattimore," October 18, 2021. https://www.missionforward.us/episodes/communicating-counter-narrative-ashton-lattimore

24 David Kestenbaum, Diane Wu, "Things I Mean to Know," *This American Life*, October 17, 2017. https://www.thisamericanlife.org/630/things-i-mean-to-know

CHAPTER 18

25 https://www.whitesupremacyculture.info/urgency.html

26 John Kotter, *A Sense of Urgency*, Harvard Business Press, January 2008.

CHAPTER 19

27 Bill Bishop, Robert Cushing, *The Big Sort: Why the Clustering of Like-Minded America is Tearing Us Apart*, May 7, 2008. http://www.thebigsort.com

28 American Psychological Association, "People Sometimes Seek the Truth, but Most Prefer Like-Minded Views" [Press Release] July, 2009. https://www.apa.org/news/press/releases/2009/07/like-minded

CHAPTER 21

29 Shankar Vedantam, Harry Reis "Relationships 2.0: What Makes Relationships Thrive," *Hidden Brain*, November 2022 https://hiddenbrain.org/podcast/what-makes-relationships-thrive/

CHAPTER 22

30 Katie Rogers, "Catalog Interview With Gloria Steinem Has Lands' End on Its Heels," *The New York Times*, February 29, 2016. http://www.nytimes.com/2016/03/01/business/catalog-interview-with-gloria-steinem-has-lands-end-on-its-heels.html?

31 The *Mission Forward* podcast, "Giving Meaning to the Word Justice with Jim Knight," April 7, 2022. https://www.missionforward.us/episodes/giving-meaning-to-the-word-justice-with-jim-knight

32 Jay Livingston, "Lands' End and the Tricky Politics of Business," *Pacific Standard Magazine*, June 14, 2017. https://psmag.com/economics/lands-end-and-the-tricky-politics-of-business

CHAPTER 24

33 Businesssolver, "Businessolver Finds Workplaces Still Lack Empathy," May 18, 2017. https://www.businessolver.com/resources/state-of-workplace-empathy

34 Her Corner, n.d. https://HerCorner.org/

35 Greater Good in Action, "Shared Identity," n.d. http://ggia.berkeley.edu/practice/shared_identity

CHAPTER 25

36 Gail Thornton, "Authentic Communication: What Does It Mean, Why It's Important," Medium, October 28, 2018. https://medium.com/thrive-global/authentic-communication-what-does-it-mean-why-its-important-51bccc80a008

Index

H

I

J

K

L

Gratitude

To every person who participated in the making of this book, I thank you.

To Brian, my love, who reads every single thing I write and always tells me if it's okay and if it's not. B.Fox, thanks for making me a better writer and giving me the courage to find my words.

To Don Foley, my mentor, friend, and most trusted counsel. So many of the ideas in this book started as conversations with you. Thanks for seeing something in me that I have a hard time seeing in myself.

To my daughters Sophia and Kate, whose questions can be as innocent as they are impossible to answer. Your curiosity and kindness inspire a deeper curiosity and kindness in me, too.

To Fred, for always keeping my lap warm on the most challenging of writing days.

To my partners and colleagues at Mission Partners and all those who contribute to making Mission Partners a truly special place to spend my days. You inspire me with your wisdom, your warmth, and your courageous leadership.

To the early readers of this manuscript, particularly Fern Fernandez and Stefanie Weiss, whose feedback inspired some of my favorite parts of this book.

To every client, past and present, that has invested in me, believed in me, and partnered with me along this path to build more just and equitable outcomes. I am honored every day to be in community and partnership with you, and I'm so proud of what we've done together.

To my editor Amy Pattee Colvin. Thanks for being my guide and partner in this book-writing journey. And to Anne Kerns who captured the spirit of my words so perfectly on the cover and inside each page.

To Mauricio Miller, Natalie Burke, Deepti Rohatgi, Ashton Lattimore, Alicia Bell, Leonard Burton, and all those who inspire me with their courage of conviction and their challenging of the norms. This book is a love letter to you.

And to my mom, whose heartful approach to life and lifelong learning inspires me daily.

About the Author

Carrie Fox is a nationally recognized leader in social impact communications and a champion for business as a force for good. She is the founder and CEO of Mission Partners, a social impact communications firm and Certified B Corporation that counsels organizations and their leaders to be more authentic in their words, equitable in their strategies, and intentional about their impact.

For the past 20 years, Carrie has guided hundreds of organizations around the world to lead with purpose, fueling organizations and their missions forward in new and more effective ways.

Carrie is a founding signatory of the #WeTheChange declaration to build business for good, and a founding member of the Purpose Collaborative, a national network of communications thought-leaders and industry experts that work together to provide dynamic problem-solving in touch with the current needs of today's purpose-driven businesses.

She is also host of the *Mission Forward* podcast, which delivers thought-provoking and perspective-shifting conversations on the power of communication. The award-winning program has featured Pulitzer Prize-winning journalists, social impact leaders, and some of the nation's most sought-after philanthropy leaders.

Carrie is a Real Leaders Impact Award winner, a Stevie Woman in Business Winner, and a past winner of *PRWeek's*

"40 under 40." She is a graduate of Loyola University Maryland, which awarded her the Ignatian Citizenship Award in 2022 for her commitment to servant leadership.

Carrie lives in Montgomery County, Maryland with her husband Brian, daughters Sophia and Kate, and their dog, Fred.

Learn more at:
www.MissionForward.us and **www.Mission.Partners**

Join Our Community

If you're ready to take your practice as a communicator for change to the next level, join our community of practice over at **www.MissionForward.us**. You'll find a podcast that brings the topics of this book to life, access to a weekly email from me that will keep you engaged in this work, and practical resources and tools to further inspire your work as a professional communicator for change.

Learn more and join us on the journey at **www.MissionForward.us**.

Thank You For Reading
More Than Words

If you found value in this book, please share your feedback. Not only will your review help us extend the reach of this book, but it will help inform my future books and projects.

Please take two minutes to leave a helpful review on Amazon, letting me know what you thought of the book. You can also join the More than Words community and access book-related events, conversations and tools at:

MissionForward.us/MoreThanWords

Thanks so much,

Carrie Fox

Notes

Made in the USA
Middletown, DE
16 May 2023

30660031R00136